T J Higgs discovered her psychic powers as a child but, owing to discouragement and a difficult upbringing, it was not until many years later that she really took flight with her gift. Today, she is one of the most successful mediums in the UK. She has appeared on TV in shows such as *Psychic Private Eyes* and *The Three Mediums*, and her work is featured widely in the media. She runs her own centre for psychic development in Essex, UK. See www.tracyhiggs.co.uk for more information.

LIVING WITH THE GIFT

T J Higgs

LONDON SYDNEY AUCKLAND JOHANNESBURG

5 7 9 10 8 6

Published in 2009 by Rider, an imprint of Ebury Publishing
A Random House Group Company

Copyright © 2009 TJ Higgs/IPM Ltd

T J Higgs/IPM Ltd have asserted their right to be identified as the authors of this
Work in accordance with the Copyright, Designs and Patents Act 1988

The Random House Group Limited Reg. No. 954009

Addresses for companies within the Random House Group can be found at
www.rbooks.co.uk

A CIP catalogue record for this book is available from the British Library

Penguin Random House is committed to a sustainable future for
our business, our readers and our planet. This book is made from
Forest Stewardship Council® certified paper.

Printed and bound in Great Britain by Clays Ltd, Elcograf S.p.A.

ISBN 9781846041952

To buy books by your favourite authors and register for offers visit
www.rbooks.co.uk

*This book tells the remarkable true story of TJ Higg's development as a medium.
However, some names and details have been changed to protect the privacy of
those involved.*

In loving memory of Hilary Goldman
and my nan Elsie.
Rest in peace. Speak soon.

Contents

Acknowledgements

When I was starting out as a psychic and a medium, my teachers and mentors often told me that I would one day write a book about my life. Deep down I never believed them. The fact that it has finally happened is largely down to the support, love and professional encouragement I've received from a very special group of people. I want to take this opportunity to thank them.

At Rider, Judith Kendra and Sue Lascelles have been fantastic supporters, guiding me through this exciting new world of publishing.

I must also say a big thank you to Garry Jenkins aka my literary spirit guide David! Thank you for all your support and for keeping my story true to me. At my management company IPM, I would like to thank the two people who continue to guide my career, Craig Goldman, who will always be my hero, and Claire Baylin, with whom I have shared so much laughter and so many tears. Thank you both. Most of all though, I have to thank Hil, Hilary Goldman, who changed my life. I will never forget you.

I also want to thank all the mediums who have taught me along the way especially the gorgeous Leah Bond who put me firmly back on my path.

I would also like to thank Colin Fry, for being a great friend and mentor, Tony Lewis, my tour manager and friend. Oh, and of course, Julian Guest, for lighting me up!

On a more personal note, I also want to thank my dear friend Marilanda for all the healing, chats we've had and all the comfort she's provided me along my rocky path. Thank you too for all the beautifying.

My final thanks, however, must go to those closest to home. Thanks to my mum and dad, for being themselves and my wonderful nan Elsie, who died on 28 March 2009, aged 91, just as I was completing this book. Last but certainly not least, thanks to my two beautiful sons James and Ryan and to Jeremy. Thank you for loving the real me.

TJ xxx

Prologue

She wasn't much more than thirty years old, but the stress lines on her face made her look at least ten years older. Her hair was a mess, and she was wearing a worn-out cardigan and no make-up. It was as if she'd given up on herself, which, in a way, she had.

It was getting towards the end of an evening show at a large theatre in the south of England and the lady had stood up and taken the microphone towards the back of the packed auditorium. A few moments earlier I'd started describing a young to middle-aged man who had passed over to the spirit world less than a year earlier. His name was David, and as he connected with me on stage I felt he had passed suddenly of a heart attack or stroke.

I could feel that David was terribly anxious to make contact with his wife, Sarah. He knew that his death had hit her hard. He was worried that she was not going to survive without him.

It was soon clear that this lady was Sarah.

As I began to talk to her through David, she confirmed his worst fears. David's sudden death had devastated her emotionally and financially. Since his passing the house they had shared together had been repossessed. She and their four children had been forced to live in a hostel, surviving on benefits.

'He can see you're struggling to keep it all together,' I said.

'I am,' she nodded gently. 'But I don't know for how much longer.'

I could see the anticipation in her eyes as she waited for some guidance from her husband. Her face lightened a little when he told me how much he had loved her and how happy she had made him. He said how proud he was of the way she was coping with their four children, despite everything. He apologised that he had left her in such a bad situation financially, and that he hadn't made proper provisions for his passing so early in life. He hoped she could forgive him for that.

'I do,' she said, almost whispering into the microphone.

But the most important message he wanted to pass on was about the future not the past.

'He is saying don't give up hope,' I said. 'David is telling you that things will get better. He's sure they will. As long as you and the children stick together and you believe in yourself.'

By now the tears had come and she was dabbing quietly away with her handkerchief. 'Thank you,' she said quietly, as she handed back the microphone and sat down.

Compared with some of the powerful messages I have relayed over the years during the course of my performances on stage, it probably didn't seem that significant, certainly to the audience. It wasn't dramatic or revelatory in any way, as some messages can be. But for me it resonated very powerfully indeed, so much so that as I began to lose the connection to David I asked Sarah to come and talk to me afterwards.

She nodded and said she would.

People often say they will come to see me after a show but then, for whatever reason, get cold feet. Sometimes they have their busy lives to get on with, of course. So I was pleased when I saw Sarah at the back of the queue for autographs after the curtain came down. She waited patiently as the long line of people dwindled away, and we were soon left alone to talk as the staff began cleaning up the theatre.

'I just wanted to tell you that I do know what you're going through,' I said.

'Do you?' she said, slightly taken aback, a questioning look on her face.

I'm a psychic but I didn't need to be one to know exactly what she was thinking. She had just watched me standing on the stage of a large theatre, dressed in an elegant evening dress and a pair of very expensive high-heels, performing to an audience of more than a thousand people, each of them having paid handsomely for the privilege of being there. She was probably thinking, quite rightly as it happens, that I was going home in a nice car to a nice big house. 'What on earth do you know about what I've been through?' she was saying to herself, although she was far too polite to come out with those exact words.

'What if I told you that not so long ago, three-and-a-half years in fact, I was exactly where you are, living in a hostel for the homeless with my two sons?' I said.

'Really?' she said. 'That's hard to believe.'

'I know. And what if I told you that I got so low and felt so depressed at what I'd done to my boys that I thought about killing myself.'

She looked shocked and said nothing.

'And what if I told you that it wasn't the first time I felt that desperate. That when I was seven I would hide in a cupboard because I was so scared of being hit by grown-ups. And that when I was a teenager I was so unhappy I ran away from home and never went back.'

I still don't think she could quite believe me but that didn't matter. I just wanted her to understand the message that her husband had been trying to get through to her.

'That's why David found you through me tonight,' I said. 'I didn't give up when I was in your position, although God knows I wanted to. Now I know there was a reason for that. I was meant to do what I'm doing now. I was given a gift and I was meant to stand on that stage tonight and use it to get that message across to you.'

With this I saw Sarah's body language change every so slightly. A small spark of determination suddenly lit up her eyes.

'There's a reason why you've got to carry on too. I didn't give up and you mustn't give up either,' I said.

We chatted for a few more minutes, this time with her telling me more about herself and her situation. The more she talked, however, the more she seemed to gain in resolve and strength.

'No. You're right,' she said at one point. 'David's right. I'm not going to give in.'

We could probably have stood there for an hour chatting, but the lights were being dimmed in the foyer. The theatre staff were locking up. It was time to go home.

We said our goodbyes outside. She said she had enough money – just – to get a bus home. Her children were waiting up for her.

As I watched her disappearing into the night, I hoped it marked the beginning of her journey back from the brink. At the same time, as I walked back to my car, I couldn't help reflecting on my own journey. I began remembering the long, eventful, sometimes painful path that had led me here to this theatre – and to Sarah – tonight.

She wasn't the only one who didn't quite believe it had happened. I wasn't entirely sure I believed it myself....

1 | A Difficult Start

The spirit world is at work around us all the time. It's constantly passing on messages, offering signs, guiding all of us as we make our way through this earthly life.

As a psychic medium, I have been blessed with the ability to pass these communications on, to help get these messages through to those for whom they are intended. It's a gift I take very seriously indeed. I have to. It took me a long time to discover it.

A lot of mediums understand their gift when they are young and spend their entire lives developing it. Mediumship is their life. For me it was different. I had a life, and then I became a medium.

I still find it ironic to think that, for the first thirty years of my life, I had absolutely no understanding of the spirit world. To be honest, I didn't know it existed, let alone that it was communicating with me, as I now believe it was, on a regular basis.

Yet I don't regret this at all. I wouldn't be the person, or the medium, I am today unless I'd had the experiences I had when I was younger. To understand and sympathise with the pain others are going through, I believe that we need to have experienced some of the setbacks and something of the pain that they are going through for ourselves.

Of course, I'd be lying if I said there hadn't been times when I wondered how my life would have turned out if I had discovered my gift earlier. Apart from anything else, I might have saved myself a lot of heartache.

I was born in Enfield in north London in January 1970. My dad Terence, or Terry as everyone knew him, had grown up locally. My mother Deirdre, or Paddy as her friends knew her, was from County Meath in Ireland.

At first we lived on Lee Road in a maisonette with a nice garden in which we kept a big white rabbit. But in 1973, when my little brother Terence – my family wasn't very imaginative with names – arrived, we moved to a bigger house on Burlington Road. It was a family street with 1930s terraced houses with big bay windows. Ours was a large, airy house, and I had a lovely, spacious bedroom. It was a really light house; in fact, I remember it always being the brightest and most full of light of all the houses along that street.

We were a big, close family. My dad's mother and father, my nan Elsie and granddad, Stanley, as well as my dad's grandfather James, my Pops, as I called him, lived in the same house, on Walton Street, around the corner from us. My mother's brother, Patrick, had married my father's sister, Pauline, and lived nearby too.

I spent a lot of time at my nan's house and regarded her as my mother in many ways. If my mother was out, as she was a lot, I would go there after school and spend time with my nan, grandad and Pops.

My memories of my nan's house are warm, something that can't be said of the house on Burlington Road.

I was really into animals as a little girl and loved dogs in particular. Once, while we were living in Burlington Road, I was bitten by an Alsatian in the street outside. I learned to be a bit more careful around dogs after that.

I got into more trouble when I found a hedgehog in the garden one day. I wanted to pick it up and care for it, so I brought it into the house. For some reason I put it under my mother's bed, thinking she'd appreciate it. She didn't. She had a very strong, Irish temper and she went nuts. I remember her telling me that hedgehogs had fleas. I was only very little at the time but it was already obvious that I couldn't do anything to please my mother.

I only have a few strong memories of that time in my life.

When Terence came home from hospital, I remember the midwives arriving to look after him in the front room. I have a powerful memory of him crying and screaming while he was in there with these women. I remember being cross and standing in the hallway shouting at them because I thought they were hurting my little brother.

They obviously weren't; they were probably stripping or washing him, but from day one I was very protective of him. In time, that protective instinct would grow stronger and stronger.

My mother wasn't always very good at coping with children. This became even more the case after she had Terence, so my nan looked after me more and more. I would always be dropped off there after school, and then picked up by my dad as he came home from work.

I consistently remember my dad looking after me. He was always working really hard, building up his own industrial spraying and French polishing business. And yet, if I look at pictures from the time he was invariably there at my nan's house. Apart from a few baby pictures of me sitting on her lap, I don't have any pictures of me with my mum when I was a girl, which was odd.

It wasn't a hardship for me to be left at my nan's house all the time. Far from it. I loved being there. My great-grandfather – my Pops – used to have pigeons in the garden. It was a big tradition in the family. All the men took up pigeon racing, including my dad.

It seems weird thinking back, but Pops believed that it tamed pigeons if you put young children in the loft with them. I have a vivid memory of me sitting on his lap and him lifting me into the large lofts with the pigeons. I can still hear them cooing away. It didn't go down well with my mother though. She used to dress me in white a lot.

The first big trauma of my young life was losing my Pops. I was three or four at the time, just a little dot.

A few memories of the day he passed will always live with me. The first one is my reaction when my mother told me the news that he was dead. 'He's not dead,' I yelled in reply, as if she were lying to me, which in an innocent way, she was. To me he wasn't dead. Somehow I sensed his spirit was still alive.

I also remember how they tried to stop me going in to see him the day he died. I can remember kicking the door to the room where he was laid out. I screamed all day long until I eventually got myself in there. When I did I climbed into the bed and just lay there with him.

The main thing I remember, though, is that his passing

marked not just my first experience of death, but my first experience of what comes after death. It was clear even then that I sensed there was something beyond death. I knew there must be more, because I saw the spirit of my Pops in the house again.

I didn't go to the funeral, but I was at my nan's house for the get-together afterwards. The whole family was there.

I saw my Pops sitting quietly in the corner, watching everyone milling around in their black suits and dresses. He seemed peaceful and content, as if he didn't have a care in the world. I remember it being a great comfort to me. I smiled at him and he smiled back.

I continued to see him in the days that followed. He would be around the house all the time and I used to talk openly to him. One day, I was playing in the living room and could see Pops sitting in his favourite armchair, as he often did. When someone came in and went to sit on the chair I let out the most almighty scream.

Not all of my family were comfortable with this. My nan didn't mind so much. When I used to tell her about seeing my Pops she just nodded. She was interested in things like reading tea-leaves, and always used to say I had 'second sight'.

My mother, on the other hand, didn't approve at all. She came from a strong Irish–Catholic background. When she heard about me shouting because someone had sat on Pops in his chair she told me in no uncertain terms that I wasn't to behave that way. I wasn't to talk about spirits any more. It was clear she disapproved of it strongly. I don't think she went as far as to say I was evil, but I'm sure that's what she was thinking.

It was confusing for me to be told I had to deny

something that seemed so real. I remember thinking for a while that it had all been in my imagination. For a long time I put it to the back of my mind. There were plenty of other things to worry about.

Within a few months of losing Pops I suffered another, even more painful, loss: my father left us.

Looking back on it, I can see now that my mother and father weren't meant to be together. They had both been young when they'd met. My mum had been seventeen when she had me, my father just twenty-one. I don't think they would have had a lasting relationship if the pregnancy hadn't happened. They were forced to marry and I think they both resented it.

One of the other memories of the house in Burlington Road is of the rows and arguments my parents used to have. I remember my mother screaming a lot.

One day I heard some shouting then a sort of repeated banging and bumping sound. I came out of my room and saw my mother lying at the bottom of the stairs.

It was after Terence had been born, so it's possible it was post-natal depression, I suppose. But whatever it was, she had taken some tablets and thrown herself down the stairs. Dramas like that were quite regular. You never knew what she was going to do next, to be honest.

Looking back on it now, I can see that it was attention seeking. Of course it wasn't our attention she was seeking – it was my father's.

It all came to a head one morning, when we were having breakfast. I remember it vividly, as if it was yesterday.

My dad had made me breakfast – Weetabix with warm milk. The warm milk had left a skin on the top of the Weetabix, and I was looking at it unsure whether I wanted to eat it.

As I was sitting there, my father leaned over me and kissed me on the head. I can still remember the smell of him as he did so. He then said goodbye. Just that. Goodbye.

Even though I was only four, I think I knew he was leaving for good. It might sound strange. I knew he wasn't just going to work. I knew he wasn't coming home. I don't think that was what my nan called my 'second sight'. It was just a child's instinct.

I didn't cry, but it did upset me a lot. I remember I didn't eat my breakfast and my mother told me off for it. It's funny; I still can't eat cereal with warm milk to this day. It still recalls that memory of my dad leaving.

From then on everything just changed. We couldn't carry on living in the big house in Enfield so my mother, brother and I moved to a much smaller flat, a few miles away in Edmonton.

I soon learned that my father had gone to live with another woman, Heather, who had separated from her husband. At the time I wasn't happy about this. But I still looked forward to the times when he came to visit us in Edmonton.

Our new flat had big windows overlooking the green in front of the block. On the days when my dad came to visit us Terence and I would watch him coming through the glass. Then when he dropped us off again we would watch him go, driving off in his car.

Even though it had that big window, it always seemed

dark in that flat. Whereas the house in Enfield always seemed full of light, I don't remember there being much light at all in Edmonton. It felt like a dark time, I suppose.

The move had an impact on us all, in particular on my mother. She couldn't cope with him not being there. We had a nice flat but she didn't have any friends. So the way she made her friends was by going to the pub. That's how I remember my mother during that time in my life. She liked drinking, so she was either in the pub or bringing loads of people back to the living room from the pub.

On Sundays she would cook dinner for a room full of people who were strangers as far as I was concerned.

I would stay in the other room, entertaining my baby brother. There was also a cupboard in the hallway, which I used to hide in, trying to get away from everyone, especially when there were lots of men in the house, which was quite often.

They were always very loud. I remember a man called Charlie in particular, who was older than my mother; he used to come around and make a lot of noise. He always smelled of beer and fags. I dreaded him calling round; he was horrible.

I don't want to give the impression that my mother was a bad woman. She wasn't. The way I look at it now is that she was a woman who was still in her early twenties, she had two kids, was in a foreign country, and living off benefits probably. It wasn't a good situation. She was trying to get over what had been a huge blow to her when my father left. I don't hate her for that. I feel sorry for her.

It fell to me to look after Terence a lot of the time. My mother would often stick his bottle in my hand then put on her coat and go out. The bottle wasn't always enough to satisfy him, of course, so I had to try to find other things for us to eat. I didn't do very well. I couldn't cook so I used to give Terence sugar sandwiches. He reminded me about it years later when all his teeth had fallen out.

I suppose it was inevitable that people were going to notice things weren't quite right. We were left to fend for ourselves a lot, and it became my job to change Terence's nappies. Auntie Pauline turned up one day and discovered me bathing my brother because his nappy had been dirty. My mother wasn't there, of course. Pauline was shocked because the water was freezing cold, but I told her that we were used to that. (In fact, until the age of ten or so my brother would always wash in freezing cold water, because that's what he'd been accustomed to as a baby.) Pauline just stood there, shaking her head. I don't think she knew what to say to us.

My mum was quite violent. As I said, she's got an Irish temper, and I took the brunt of her stress and her anger at my father leaving.

'I didn't want a little girl, I wanted a little boy,' she'd shout at me. 'Your dad wouldn't have left me if I'd had a boy.'

She was dealing with a lot of emotions in her head because my father had fallen out of love with her and fallen in love with someone else. As I say, I really do feel sorry for her now.

She was always disapproving and I used to be terrified of disappointing her. I remember once going to a shop near a place called Pymms Park in Edmonton. To get there you had to go through a car park and garages, and down an alleyway. This was when I was six or so. I wouldn't let a fifteen-year-old walk down there alone. But she would send me with no thought.

If I forgot anything, when I got back she would kick off; she would go completely mad – verbally, violently.

On this particular occasion, it wasn't the normal backhander or 'you're stupid'. She picked me up and threw me on the bed then picked up the Hoover and threw that at me. I remember it really well. I remember lying on the bed thinking, 'I'm not going to move'. My feet were tingling, my body was hurting, but I thought, 'I'm not going to move'. You get to that point where you don't feel pain.

I was afraid to say anything.

Something similar happened when I ended up in hospital. The official story was that a clock fell on top of me from a shelf. But the truth was different.

As I lay in bed I was asked a lot of questions by the doctors and nurses. I think that's when my dad realised what was going on.

I don't know why, but my mother seemed to direct her anger more at me than my little brother. It was an unhappy time and I dealt with it as a lot of children do, by retreating into my own fantasy world.

I know a lot of mediums write about seeing unicorns and all that kind of stuff when they were children, but it wasn't like that for me. I went off to a fantasy world where there were horses and fairies. I had always loved horses. I didn't see it as mediumistic thing. It was a normal little girl's thing. It was where I went to be safe. I had to have somewhere where I felt safe.

The final straw came when Terence nearly burned the house down. I don't think you can blame a four-year-old for getting up to things. A child is allowed to get up to things. The problem was that, unlike other children who are obsessed with toys or television, my brother loved fire. He learned how to burn things. I guess you would have called him a pyromaniac.

The first time it happened was when he decided that he was going to burn the little park we had in front of the flats. It wasn't so much a park as a fenced off bit of grass. He managed to crawl in there and set it alight one day with matches. I don't know how he did it. He was a naughty little so-and-so.

Then one day he decided to take it a step further.

Looking back I think I can understand what was going on in his young mind. We had been watching a cowboy film on television. The cowboys had built a campfire, and to stop it spreading beyond a certain point they had put powder round it.

My brother had seen this and thought he'd do something similar – in my bedroom. So he'd got some toothpaste and squeezed a big white circle around my bed, inside which he piled up my toys and my dolls. He'd then set fire to it all.

The problem was that it was night time. My mother was out and I was in the bed. The first thing I knew of what was going on was when I woke up and found myself being carried out of a window by a fireman. I also remember being covered in toothpaste. He had obviously wanted me to be safe too.

It wasn't long afterwards that I went to live with my dad.

My dad had seen enough to know that I couldn't go on living with my mother, but it wasn't that straightforward, of course.

The case had to go through the courts before it was agreed that I went to live with my father. I remember my dad telling me I might have to stand up in court and say that I wanted to leave. He and my step-mum did go to court, but I don't remember ever having to do so myself.

My brother remained living with my mother, though. He would come to visit me and my dad at the weekends. We'd drop him off back with my mother, and he used to cry at the big double window – screaming for me.

I can still see his face.

Within a year or so of me moving out he had joined us. My mother went to visit her family in Ireland for a short time, and while she was away he stayed with us. Then we just got a phone call telling us that she was going over for longer and telling us to come and collect his things.

I learned a lot later that originally it was my mother's plan to take both my brother and me to Ireland with her. That didn't happen, thank goodness. But she didn't stay in Ireland and, when she was back, she would come and see us on Sundays. That was our day with her.

When I was with her, she used to quiz me in the way that parents do when they are divorced or separated. I remember her being obsessed with it. She was also unreliable.

Sometimes she would say she was going to come and then not show up.

When she didn't show up it hurt. I can't pretend any different.

I remember on Mother's Day in 1979, when I was nine years old, she was meant to come and see us. On the Saturday I got my pocket money together and went out to buy a present each for my step-mum and my mother. I bought my step-mum a plant from the florists and I bought my mother a little figurine of a family of squirrels. There was a big squirrel, a medium one and then a baby one. In my head, they represented her, me and my brother.

But she never turned up. It was then that I started to feel that I never wanted her back in my life again because of the way she'd hurt me.

Even as a nine-year-old I had forgiven her for everything she had done. I had forgiven her for hitting me all the time, I had forgiven her for leaving us to go and get drunk with all those men in the pub all the time, even for boyfriends of hers beating me around the room. But I couldn't forgive her for that – not turning up.

That Mother's Day I gave the second present to my step-mum instead. The family of squirrels stayed in the house for a long time but my brother, mother and I were never a family again. That was the last my brother and I heard of my mother for many, many years. She never came round to see us again.

As a mother myself, I can't imagine not wanting to be around my children. I can't get that into my head – it just doesn't make sense to me. Your children are a part of you. Even rationalising how my own mother was, and the fact that she was trying to make a new life for herself, nothing would stop me getting to my children. I would have fought through the courts. But none of that ever happened.

I later learned that eventually they decided to keep my mother away from me because she wasn't a very good influence. My father and step-mum had decided she was too disruptive. They weren't going to have my brother and I sitting there in the window wondering whether she was going to turn up every Sunday. They had said, 'enough'.

Above all, I see now that the experiences I went through had a purpose. I came through them so that I could help others come through similar experiences. Today, I regard the difficult times I endured with my mother as a positive thing. It often provides me with a way of helping others deal with their difficult relationships.

That was certainly the case when I first began reading for a lady I'll call Sandie. Sandie was married to a very handsome Italian man who was devoted to her – as she was to him. She was devastated when he died of cancer at quite a young age.

Fortunately, I found that I was able to communicate with him fairly easily. Since Sandie started coming to me for readings he has regularly come to talk to her. We sit down with a nice glass of Italian red wine and she keeps him up to date with her life. She finds it a huge comfort.

When I first began reading for Sandie, however, I discovered that there was always another presence. It was a woman. And the feelings she was giving out were very different to those of Sandie's husband.

The first time this happened I was taken back to my childhood and that sense I always had of not being wanted. As a psychic and a medium, I have the ability to sense many things. One of the things I can tell immediately is whether or not someone was brought up by their real mother.

So it proved here. I sensed this was Sandie's mother, although she didn't have a maternal feeling about her daughter at all. When I asked Sandie whether she'd been brought up by someone other than her mother she nodded. She then told me that her family had taken her away from her birth mother when she was a baby. Another member of the family had raised her, because for some reason her mother hadn't been able to care for her. She had never known what that reason was. Nor had she known who her father was.

I found it hard to deal with this woman's presence. She didn't want to make the peace or make amends in any way – that was clear. She hadn't come through to me to offer any apologies for what she'd done. There was no remorse. There was no relationship with her daughter at all really.

But as I began to read for Sandie on a regular basis her presence began to bear fruit. One of the first things I got from her was confirmation that she had in fact walked away from Sandie when she was a baby. The family had been telling stories to protect Sandie. The truth was her mother had abandoned her.

This was hard at first, but eventually Sandie saw it as a comfort and a relief that she knew the truth. It confirmed what she'd felt instinctively all her life.

As she got to know this spirit, she also began to understand a lot more about herself. She realised she too could be emotionally detached. She could see that she got that from her mother. Her mother told her how headstrong she could be at times too, something else that Sandie recognised.

She had never seen a photograph of her mother or read a word she'd written in a letter. The readings helped her fill in some of the gaps that childhood experience had left in her heart. They went some way towards healing her childhood wounds.

I consider it a great privilege to be able to help people in this way. And I know I wouldn't be able to do it unless I understood something of how they felt. In this particular case, I had a pretty good idea what Sandie was feeling because it brought back the emotions I'd gone through myself. Every time I sensed her mother I felt that familiar nagging doubt that I'd had in my head when I was a child. 'Why didn't she want me?' 'Why did she leave?' 'What was wrong with me?'

To turn such a negative into a positive has been a huge blessing in my life. It has been as healing for me as it has been for many of the people who I've connected to the spirit world.

The contrast between my mother and my step-mum – or my mum, as I eventually came to call her – couldn't have been greater.

When I first went to live with them, my dad and Heather had a flat on a council estate in Enfield. She had been married before as well and had three children: Amanda, Colin and Peter, who were all there too.

The first memory I have of going there was of Heather

making chocolate éclairs. I remember her bringing the éclairs out of the oven and the sweet, warm smell of the cake filling the air.

I had never seen a mother doing that.

Living with her was so different from living with my mother. With my mother, I never knew what I was going to find in the house each morning, or even who was going to be there. With my step-mum there was a routine; we were given chores.

We didn't live in that flat for long. It was a council property, but then my dad bought a house in Halifax Road, Enfield, which he planned on extending. It had a garden and lots of space.

When we moved there we got a dog that it was my job to take out into the garden. She was lovely little Jack Russell, called Pepsi. I could sit in the garden and talk to her for hours on end. My dad also had pigeons, which needed looking after. Later on we kept chickens, which, again, needed attention. There was always a sense of responsibility, which I never had in my mum's house. In my childlike mind, I decided that my step-mum was a proper mum.

I also felt safer there.

My dad was very protective. I remember after dad finished the extension my sister Amanda and I had a bigger room. One day I remember my nextdoor neighbour climbing up a ladder and looking into my bedroom and me shouting at him. My dad was in the garden and he went for him straight away. He was my hero, there to protect me, which was never a feeling I had with my mother.

My relationship with my step-mum wasn't always easy though during those first years. It was never going to be, I suppose. Being separated from my mother was like a bereavement in a way. It was very hard, especially at school where there were girls with their mums all the time. It wasn't that my stepmother wasn't a good mum, because she looked after me really well. But it didn't matter how much she looked after me she still wasn't my real mother. With the best will in the world she couldn't fill that void inside me.

If your mother doesn't want you, you don't get over that. It doesn't matter if you have an amazing woman take over; it doesn't matter what your stepmother is like – she is still not your mum. And I think I've felt that all my life.

I can remember lying in my room asking those endless questions. 'Why didn't my mum want me? Why did she leave us? Dads leave but mums don't. What was wrong with me? Was it my fault my mum and dad had split up?' The result was inevitable, I suppose.

I know I wasn't an easy child. I was bloody hard work. Part of this was down to the fact that I was used to being beaten and I was on edge all the time. So I reacted before I should.

I remember one day my step-mum sent me out to the Chinese restaurant to get some food. I didn't realise there were two of them and I'd gone to the wrong one and brought the wrong food home.

I didn't know that until Heather started unpacking the meal and she was suddenly raising her voice. 'Tracy, you silly girl! You've gone and got the wrong food,' she said.

To me, the fact she'd raised her voice meant she was going to beat me, so I ran from our house all the way to our nan's, petrified. My dad had to come and get me.

Because of the way I was and the experiences I'd had, we had quite a few problems settling down as a new family. It was easier for my brother, I think, because he was so young, just three, when he made the move. It was harder for me.

Part of it was the normal stuff of childhood. I had to share my room with my step-sister Amanda – Mandy as she was called – and she would do things, then blame me for having done them. She was four years older than me. It was just what kids do, but at the time I found it really hard because I thought it meant they didn't want me there.

Their mother had left a bad marriage too, it turned out. In time I realised that my father and Heather really were meant to be together. They are still together today, thirty-five years later. Peter, Colin and Mandy's father was on the scene for a while. He remarried and had children as well. We used to go there to visit them. His new wife was there.

It only made my own mother's absence from my life harder to understand. If the other children were allowed to go and see their father, why weren't we allowed to see our mother, I used to think.

There was no question, though, that living with my dad gave me the stability that I'd lacked when I was with my mother. But when he enrolled me in the local school, Chase Side Primary, I was very much a loner. I couldn't talk to anybody properly and I found it very hard to connect with anyone emotionally, especially children of my age.

Yet the funny thing was that, while I felt alone physically, I didn't feel completely alone. I really had no understanding of what it meant at the time.

2 | Growing Up Guided

Looking back at my childhood with the benefit of hindsight, I can see now that there were a few clues pointing to the life I was eventually going to lead. I didn't know it at the time, but I was definitely someone who saw the world differently – often quite literally.

From a young age I could see the energy in the air, for instance. It was more than just seeing a heat haze on a summer's day or the dust in the air when a bright shard of light breaks through a window. When I looked at someone or something I could actually see the particles of the air moving in front of me. It was a pure white energy.

I didn't know what it was then, but I do now. I was seeing the energy and the auras of living things. I would often spend time just sitting watching it all, without trying to make sense of what it meant.

I could also pick up on the emotions and feelings these auras were giving off. Again, I didn't understand what it all meant then. I just assumed it was something that everyone could do.

For instance, if someone was lying or was somehow out to hurt me I would see the area surrounding their eyes turning dark. Now, of course, I tell them I'm a psychic. 'So why bother lying to me?' I joke. But back then I had no idea I was blessed with this ability.

It was only many years later that it dawned on me what this signalled. It all fell into place when I had an experience with a boyfriend who was blatantly lying to me. As he spoke I noticed that he had this distinct, black mark around his eyes, as if he'd had soot rubbed into his face. He looked a bit like a panda.

It was then that the penny dropped. When I saw it, all sorts of memories from my childhood came flooding back. In an instant all the people who had lied or cheated on me when I was a kid came into my mind.

I remembered, for instance, how my mother's eyes would darken when she talked to me sometimes. When she used to tell my brother and me she'd come to see us again soon, I'd see the telltale signs.

That was why I'd known deep down that she wasn't going to come to see us on that Mother's Day. Somewhere inside me I'd known that she wouldn't come so that I could give her that little squirrel ornament. She couldn't look me in the face often; it was as if she knew I knew she was lying.

My ability to sense people's feelings went further than this. I could also sense the mood of those who were around me. Of course, everyone can do this sometimes. Often you can feel whether a person is in a good or bad mood. You don't need to be psychic to know it. But I would be able to look at the colours in their aura and work out not just whether they were in a particular mood but what had caused that mood. The first time I noticed this was with our animals.

We had got Pepsi, our Jack Russell, from the RSPCA in Potter's Bar. She was a rescue dog. She was very feisty, as Jack Russells can be. My dad's garden was 200 feet long and to restrain Pepsi we attached her to a 100-foot chain.

Pepsi was a temperamental dog and I used to be able to look at her and see her colour change with her moods. So, for instance, if she was a pale light green, I knew she was in a good mood. When she was this colour she would be all over me and was very approachable. But if her coat was a darker blue colour, I knew not to approach her. I knew I had to wait for her to come to me.

It was the same with Smokey, the bantam that I befriended when the family started keeping chickens. We hatched the bantams from eggs my dad bought in the market and then each of the children adopted one. Smokey, became my chicken.

Normally Smokey's colour was green but when she was about to lay eggs this changed ever so slightly. I would see her feathers were different shades of green, and they were shifting a lot. I quickly learned that if I saw her in that colour that she was about to disappear into one of the sheds my father kept at the bottom of the garden and lay her eggs.

Back then I had no idea why these colour changes happened, of course. But now, having studied auras and the auric field that all beings project, I understand that green is connected to what is known as the heart chakra. Chakras are energy points throughout your body that are associated with certain emotions. Green is a warm feeling, so when Pepsi was showing green, she was giving off a warm signal.

Colours are open to interpretation; people can read them in their own ways. Blue, for me, is symbolic of depression or anxiety. So when I saw that dark blue I knew Pepsi was in a less welcoming frame of mind.

This ability to see colours where others couldn't cropped up again and again during my childhood. I was a keen reader, as was my step-mum. Heather would buy a lot of those magazines you could build up monthly. She was really into crime stories and biographies of famous criminals and murderers. When she had finished with them I'd read all about these fascinating people. It was quite morbid really, although it proved useful many years later!

I remember reading about Ruth Ellis. The pictures in these magazines were always black and white, but when I looked at her I could see her face in colour. I used to think it was because I had a really good imagination, but now I wonder whether it wasn't my imagination at all. Maybe I was 'feeling' her. Many years later, in a circle, Ruth Ellis came through. I saw that same face again.

These things were showing themselves to me all the time but I told no-one. Since being reprimanded for talking about seeing my Pops, I had learned to keep my mouth firmly shut. As I settled into life in a new family, my code of silence made even more sense. If I'd shared what I was seeing and feeling with my new brothers and sisters, they would have thought I was even madder than they already did. I felt isolated enough as it was. I didn't need to make it worse.

There were other clues that I was a little bit unusual, certainly compared to the other children. I have never met anyone with the same colour eyes as me. As a child I was really conscious of their brightness and intensity and the way they could change colour. They still do.

Today, when I'm working my eyes go blurry and they change shade, usually from green to grey. I'm used to it now. People come up to me and ask me where I found my amazing coloured contact lenses. But at school it upset me when children drew attention to them, which of course they did a lot. I was teased with names like 'cats' eyes', 'witches' eyes' or 'evil eyes'. I hated it. I always wanted to wear contact lenses and I never wanted people to look at me.

It sounds strange now that I'm in the media but I didn't like to be noticed when I was young; I wasn't an attention seeker at all. The more often I could disappear, the better, really. For many years I would avert my gaze if people looked at me.

Only once did it occur to me that my eyes might mean I had abilities others didn't have. When I was around ten or eleven I was with a friend, a girl called Kelly. We had been out together, playing, and were walking back through a dark alleyway. I can't remember what it was she did but she obviously did or said something to upset me because I just glared at her.

I hadn't done it before – although I have done it again since, mainly to make a point to my boys when they were growing up. They used to call it 'the death stare'. On this occasion, it was deliberate and it obviously had an impact because Kelly burst into tears and started screaming, 'Stop staring at me like that – you're scaring me!' She ran home and I followed her. I knew her mother and father well, and her mum, Chris, pulled me to one side. 'Did you stare at her like she said?' she asked me.

'Yes, I did,' I said.

She tried to explain to me why I shouldn't do this. I think it was the first time anyone had been so honest with me about my eyes. 'You shouldn't do it because you have really piercing eyes and they can scare people,' she said.

When I was eleven or so we moved from the house on Halifax Road to a large three-storey Victorian house in Gordon Hill in Enfield. It was a much older, bigger house.

It was soon after we moved in that I sensed it was occupied by someone from the spirit world.

My mum and dad both worked so my nan used to come and clean the house during the daytime. She would come there after finishing another cleaning job around the corner.

By now Amanda was in the sixth form at school. She was also working nights in a photographic studio, processing pictures. So she would often sleep in later than the rest of us in the mornings.

Mandy woke up one morning and heard the bath upstairs running. She knew that the rest of us had gone out so she assumed it must be my nan, doing the cleaning. She went into the bathroom to see the bath was nearly full to overflowing and turned the tap off. She then called out for my nan expecting her to be there. But my nan wasn't there. And she hadn't been there all day. In fact there had been no-one in the house all day.

That really freaked Mandy out. From then on she reckoned there was something odd about the place. 'I don't like the feeling in this house,' she said to me more than once.

I didn't say anything. I was still careful not to broadcast the fact that I saw and felt things that others didn't. But when I heard Mandy talking about the running bath I knew immediately that it was the spirit that lived there. Ever since we'd moved in I'd had a feeling of being watched all the time. And I always had a strong feeling that there was another little girl in that house. I couldn't see her, but I was convinced of it.

A few years later when Mandy left home I got my own bedroom. Amanda's bed was still in the room and I always felt as if someone was sleeping in it at night, which made me feel that spiritually I wasn't alone; I liked that.

By the time I turned fifteen I knew exactly what I wanted to do with my life. My brother Peter had been toying with the idea of going into the Army and had a lot of literature about it at home. I'd read it and immediately decided this was what I wanted to do.

I had visions of being in the police force, SIB. I'd read all these books that my mum had about criminal investigations and would watch *Quincy* on TV. That was a big influence on me.

I wanted to understand people at a psychological level. There was a written test you could do to apply for entry to the Army so – despite the fact you were supposed to be seventeen – I had a go. No-one asked my age and I looked older than fifteen.

I passed the entry test with flying colours, but when they found out I was two years too young they suggested I spend some time in the Army cadets first. They told me I had to do some training, get used to the Army life. To me, that sounded perfect. I was still a tomboy rather than a girlie girl. Everyone was into *Star Wars* at the time. I loved the film too, but I wanted to be Luke Skywalker rather than Princess Leia. I joined the cadets in Cheshunt and was soon spending my weekends being a Lance Corporal.

I loved everything about it: the friends I made there, the outdoor pursuits, the routine and order of it. Perhaps it was a reflection of the disorder and chaos of my early life. The Army seemed a place where life ran according to rules.

They say you have friends that are a season, a reason and a lifetime. I've had a lot of seasons and a lot of reasons. I only have a few friends who are for a lifetime. This was mainly because I still wouldn't let many people get that close to me. That emotional barrier was still there. I was also a bit different to the other girls. I didn't need to be with the girls at the weekend, going to the pictures. I wasn't really into all that.

But when I joined the Cadets I began to make some real friends, including my best friend Bonnie. Her parents had split up too, and she was going through a lot of what I was going through. There was this feeling of trust with her straight away. We've remained friends ever since.

I had gone up to Enfield Chase Secondary School, an all-girls' school. I had continued to do well and was close to top of the class. I got on with my work, stayed out of trouble. I suppose I was quite boring really.

When school held a careers day that year I went along with a clear idea in my head. 'I want to join the Army,' I told the careers teacher.

Her reaction wasn't what I expected. She laughed then said, 'No.' This wasn't because my teachers didn't have faith in me. They did. I remember one teacher telling me that they thought I'd end up as Prime Minister. I never quite understood that.

Being stubborn and single-minded, I was now even more determined that I was going to go into the Army. But as I looked around the careers advice information available that day I found there was nothing. So I went to the library and found an address for the Brigadier in London who was in charge of Army recruitment. I wrote to the address, complaining that my school didn't have any literature about Army careers. I told them I was an Army cadet and wanted to join the Forces.

I didn't think any more of it until a couple of weeks later, when I received a letter from the Brigadier inviting me to London. He gave me a lovely lunch and then he and some others interviewed me. I didn't know what was going on really. So when they told me that they had an offer to make me, I was taken by surprise.

'We'd like you to finish school, and then go to University, at our expense,' the Brigadier explained. 'At the end you'll come straight into the Army as an officer.'

I was fifteen years old. It was a measure of how very independent-minded I was that I remember thinking I didn't want to follow this path. 'I want to go in at the bottom of the ranks and work my way up. I don't want to be privileged,' I said to myself.

The Brigadier made sure that they sent someone to our summer camp in 1986. Again, I'd made so many complaints about us women not being noticed and taken care of that they sent a female Colonel.

In little ways, I don't mean to challenge authority but I

do believe that things should be fair for everyone. No-one should be in control of you and your thoughts. It's an attitude I still have today, even after all the trouble it's got me into.

I know now that I was being guided by the spirit world even at that early age. I was being steered in the right directions by spirits watching over me. Sometimes I'm sure – without thinking – I listened. Sometimes, I know, I didn't.

As I moved through my late teens I would come to regret not listening more often.

One evening in 1986, when I was sixteen, I was at home on my own when there was a loud knock on the front door. I opened it to find a friend of mine, Joanne, in floods of tears on the doorstep.

'What's wrong?' I asked.

'It's Ian,' she sobbed. 'He just attacked me. You've got to help me. Can you come with me to his place?'

As she said this I could see the darkening around her eyes and I heard a voice in my head saying 'she's lying'.

There were normally seven people in the house but on this particular evening I was alone. I didn't know what to do. I knew Ian well. His parents were friendly with mine and they came round to our house regularly. The Ian I knew wasn't violent at all, but Joanne seemed really upset, verging on hysterical. So I said I'd walk her back up the hill to Ian's place to sort it out.

No sooner had I left the house and started walking up the hill than I was once more hearing voices: '*Stop, turn around, go home; they're going to hurt you.*'

It was like I was reading a book and hearing someone speaking the words in a voice that wasn't quite mine. I remember thinking: 'Where's that coming from, that's not normal?' But I was a bloody-minded and independent girl, and so I carried on. 'Who is going to hurt me?' I asked myself. 'And who is that talking to me, anyway?'

As I turned the corner into the street where Ian lived there were two girls there waiting for us – Jeannette and another girl called Jo. Again, I was so naïve that I didn't think anything about it. I didn't think, 'What are they doing here? How did they know we would be coming this way?' But I soon regretted my decision to help Joanne.

The next thing I knew she had turned and grabbed my hair. She then swung me around and started smacking my head against a wall, shouting all this stuff about Ian. I couldn't believe it – she was accusing me of stealing her boyfriend. She was saying that he and I were doing things behind her back when he came to visit my house.

It was only later that I discovered that to get at Joanne, Ian had been making up stories about something going on between me and him. Some friend, he proved to be.

By the time they'd finished attacking me I was bleeding heavily from the head. Somehow I walked home. Fortunately it was only three minutes or so away. My parents still weren't there. So I went to a neighbour's house where I found some friends were in. They took one look at the state of me and called an ambulance because my face was so smashed up.

I was rushed to casualty where they examined me. It turned out the girls had broken a bone in my face. The hospital was so concerned about the attack that they called in the police. I told them what had happened and, in the days that followed, they decided to press charges against the three of them. It had clearly been a premeditated attack; they had planned to get me out of the house and set about me when I least suspected it.

The problem was that all three girls were in my class at school and the police couldn't guarantee my safety. This put the school authorities in a really tricky situation.

I can remember endless meetings with my father. I gave so many statements about what had happened that I lost track of them. But then, after all that, the school made a decision that left me speechless. It was advised that I leave and not them. My father and I were really angry. In effect, I was being punished for what the three girls had done to me.

The injustice of it was bad enough, but what really annoyed me was that I was towards the top of the academic ladder at the school. Those girls were all doing CSEs and I was doing O levels. And I had every intention of staying on for the sixth form. I had the Army offer of being put through University at their expense.

They took all that away from me.

I had to leave school at the end of April and go back to do my exams in the summer. I could have enrolled at another school, I suppose, but with only weeks to go until the exams it would have been a nightmare to organise.

So I carried on studying but without any of the revision classes that were being put on at school. Inevitably, it harmed my exam chances. I was doing physics at O level and the exam required a practical test. I didn't have the dates for it because I wasn't going to school every day, so I missed the test completely. I didn't pass Physics O level because of it.

The whole episode was, looking back on it, a major turning point in my life.

On the positive side, the experience did teach me to listen the next time I heard a clear message in my head like that.

A year or so later I was walking home from Army Cadets one Sunday evening in the summer. I was going up Lavender Hill in my combats when a blue escort estate car pulled up alongside me on the other side of the road. The man inside was a skinny, slightly weasely-looking character. He was wearing jam-jar glasses. I looked at him and he looked at me. From across the road, he asked me a question, but as I couldn't hear him I went to step towards him.

As I did so all my energy changed. I was suddenly on alert; I was tingling. As I got close to the car all I could hear was somebody screaming in my head: '*Run!*' It was as clear as if someone was standing behind me. I'd learned my lesson by now. I turned and started running away immediately.

As I did so I saw him open his car door, climb out and lunge towards me. I wasn't frightened of him. I knew my martial arts from the Cadets. So I had no doubt that I could have physically fended him off. But I wasn't going to hang around. I ran all the way home.

My dad was there and I told him about it. He took down the details of the car and went straight out to look for him. We also told the police. That evening an officer came round. He told us that this man was wanted by the police, as he had approached other girls and had been known to get them into his car.

I remember thinking afterwards about these voices I'd

been hearing in my head. I'd listened to them tonight and had a lucky escape. By contrast, I'd not listened to them that evening with Joanne, and look at the trouble it had caused. I told myself I should always listen to them in future. But I didn't listen, did I?

For a long time I could only see what happened to me at school as a terrible thing. It was a dark episode, which hung over me. But in time, as with so many other events in my life, I was able to draw on that experience and use it in a positive way.

A few years ago I did a reading for a mother who lived near me. It was one of those readings where one thing seemed to dominate everything else. All I could see all the time were images of her son. He wasn't dead. But his relationship with his mother was. I felt no motherly love in her at all. I just felt pain.

It turned out that her son was in his late teens and he had gone off the rails completely, becoming uncontrollable. He had been playing truant from school, had been in trouble with his teachers and even the police. It had all come to a head and he had been kicked out of his family home. He was now living with a foster family.

I could see that this was eating up his mother. She was in a terrible state, and it was clear that she didn't want to be estranged from him. I could also sense that the boy's father was angry at what had happened. I could see the whole family was in a lot of pain.

I had a strong sense that I wanted to speak to this boy. I felt there was something missing, that there was something his mother didn't know. So, unusually for me, I decided to intervene. 'I don't know if this would help, but would you ask him if he'd come and see me?' I asked the mother. 'I'd like to find out what's at the root of this.'

She seemed quite pleased by this. She came in with her son the following Saturday afternoon. He was fourteen years old. I don't normally do readings for people under the age of eighteen because I feel that they are too young, and that they should face their future without any preconceptions. But I felt there was a reason why I needed to talk to this boy.

He didn't want to look at me at first. But when I explained that I was going to read Tarot cards and see what I could learn about his life, he was intrigued. I asked him to shuffle them and began reading. As I laid the cards out I saw immediately that this boy was being bullied horrendously at school. He was a big lad, physically speaking. But I could see that he was terrified of the other boys, even those who were smaller than him. I saw that they would gang up on him and even beat him up.

He looked shocked when I told him this. 'That's why you are bunking off school,' I explained. 'It's the only way you know how to deal with it. That's your escape.'

He nodded.

Again, it was my own personal experience of what had happened to me that allowed me to feel this so acutely and accurately. Throughout the reading I kept feeling the sense of anger and frustration and unfairness that I'd also felt at school. Like this boy I'd done nothing wrong, yet, like him, I'd been punished for it.

I explained this to him. I recounted to him what had happened to me and how I had suffered as a result. He was taken aback. I had been on television by this time and, to his eyes at least, was a strong, confident person.

'I'd never have guessed you'd been bullied like that,' he said.

'I was,' I said. 'But I faced up to it and I got on with my life. You've got to do the same. And you've got to do it with your family's help.'

Before he left I got him to make a pact with me. He promised he would go home and try again with his parents, but before that I would tell them what had happened to him. He agreed. His mother was sitting outside and I asked her in to explain what had been going on. She cried when I told her what suffering her boy had been through on his own. But she left determined to help him sort it out.

A few months later I was sitting in the reception of my centre when a man arrived with a very large bunch of flowers.

It was the boy's father. 'I want to thank you for giving me my son back,' he said.

I didn't know what to say. Fortunately, he was doing all the talking for me. 'He had no-one to listen to him. But you listened and you understood him. So we've now been able to sort everything out at school and at home. He's living back with us again.'

In those dark days when I was asked to leave school, I never imagined that anything positive would come of it. But how wrong I was. Without that experience I'd never have been able to help that family get back together. For that reason, if I went back and lived my life again, I wouldn't change a bit of it.

3 | Teenage Bride

In January 1987, I turned seventeen. I was happy with the way my life was heading. I'd decided not to go back to school for A levels and was working in the accounts department of a company on White Hart Lane in Tottenham, saving up money for when I was going to go into the Army the following year. I also had a regular boyfriend, Tony, a Yorkshireman I had met through the Cadets. He was twenty-one, four years older than me, and was a serving soldier in the Royal Signals. We were seeing each other regularly, although I didn't see it as something particularly serious.

I certainly didn't see myself marrying him. I was the same age as my mother was when she had become pregnant; I wasn't going to repeat her silly mistake. I had a very different plan mapped out for myself. At that point, marriage and children couldn't have been further from my mind. I had taken an entrance exam for the Army again and done well. So well in fact that the Army careers officer I'd spoken to had said that I would be able to pick and choose my role when I had finished my basic training. 'You will be able to do absolutely anything,' he'd said.

I already had an idea that I'd like to go into the Military Police or the Services Investigation Bureau, the CID branch of the military.

Of course the worst thing you can do is tell God your plans.

In the early spring I started having more weird dreams. I kept hearing warnings, voices saying: 'Be careful, you're going get pregnant.' Tony and I were sleeping together but we were being careful. I just thought, 'That's stupid, that's never going to happen.'

That April my step-sister Amanda turned twenty-one. My dad organised a big party at a local golf club and the whole family was invited. It was going to be a big affair so I decided to buy myself a new outfit.

I went out shopping on the Saturday before the party and tried on a few dresses. The only problem was that they were all too tight; I couldn't fit into any of them. This didn't make sense. Spending weekends doing exercises with the Cadets meant that I was fit. I shouldn't have put on any weight. In the end I bought an outfit that was a size bigger than normal, and thought nothing more of it.

On the night of the party I turned up with Tony, who was meeting the whole family for the first time. It was a big, old-fashioned family celebration. It was also the last time that I saw all my family gathered together in one place. My dad, mum, nan, brothers and sisters and all my aunts and uncles were there, having a drink, a dance and a good laugh. It was a fun night. Well, until my nan came up to me.

My nan was getting on by now and didn't stay out particularly late. As she was leaving, she came over to Tony and me. 'You had better get yourself a pram,' she said, looking me in the eye. Tony was standing beside me. We both just laughed. 'Don't laugh,' she said, 'I'm telling you you're pregnant.'

I looked at Tony and he looked at me. Suddenly it flashed through my mind what had happened the previous Saturday in the shops. And I knew she was right.

All the same, I didn't want to believe it. So I just ignored it. The next weekend I went away, as planned, on an adventure-training weekend with the Cadets. I spent two days running, climbing and tackling assault courses. I slept out under canvas. I didn't even consider what I could be doing to the child I might be carrying.

But then one morning the following week, as I was heading to work, I felt really ill. I knew what it meant and decided I had to face up to it by going to see a doctor. I rang in sick for work and made an appointment to see our local GP. This was only twenty or so years ago, but things were very different then. Pregnancy testing kits weren't that common. Most people still went to the doctor to have an examination. Sure enough the doctor confirmed what my nan had seen. I was in the early stages of pregnancy.

I decided not to tell anyone, apart from Tony. In my mind, I had good reason to be secretive. First and foremost, I knew my father would go ballistic. I also dreaded having to face my nan, and hearing her tell me, 'I told you so!'

But I was also frightened they were going to make me have an abortion. As much as I hadn't planned on having a baby, I simply couldn't envisage getting rid of it. I can see now that a lot of that was to do with not wanting to recreate my mother's situation.

The minute I knew I was pregnant I also knew that I didn't want my baby to feel unwanted in the way that I had done. I felt as if I was protecting him even before he was born. So from the beginning I didn't have any thoughts about not having my child. I couldn't have done it. I didn't want my baby to feel rejected.

Of course, I knew I couldn't keep it a secret forever. Living in a house with other women, in particular, meant I couldn't hide the telltale signs for very long. Eventually I was forced to admit the truth.

Tony and I tried to tell my parents on two occasions but it just didn't work out. It wasn't the right time. I was really panicking about telling my dad. In the end I told Heather, my step-mum. She just looked at me and pointed towards a chair in the kitchen. 'You had better sit there until your father gets home,' she said.

I can't repeat what my father's first words were when I told him. It was devastating to see his reaction as the news sank in. It was the way his face looked that hurt the most. The expression on his face was more than disappointment – it was utter emptiness. I was his little girl and, to him, I was throwing away my life. I had done well at school and I had a great career in the Army ahead of me. In hindsight, I can't blame him for feeling that way at all. If I'd been in his shoes I'd have been the same.

I remember that his expression went from shock to anger after a while. He picked himself up and walked out in to the garden where he lit up a cigarette. He stayed out there for ages.

The news hit the house like a bombshell. The atmosphere became horrible and we were soon having awful arguments at home.

As I feared, my parents raised the idea of me having a termination. They were frightened that I wouldn't have a life after the child was born. As a mother, I totally understand that now, but I was on the other side of the fence then and I was determined that I was going to take control of my life. Not them.

Things came to a head one day when my mum took me to a meeting at Chase Farm Hospital. I had already had the first scans and general medical check-ups to make sure that the baby and I were both OK. Everything seemed fine. This was a meeting with my mum, me and a social worker.

The social services people were trying to find out where I was going to live with the baby, whether I needed any accommodation – the practical details. But as we sat there discussing my future it was my mum who did all the talking. 'We don't know if she is going to have this baby, and we don't know if we are going to raise it for her,' she said at one point.

There was this important conversation going on about my and the baby's future and yet it was as though I wasn't really a part of it. It was as if I wasn't there. I kept thinking: 'Hold on a minute, it's me having the baby, I'm sitting here'. So I just left the room and went outside into the corridor. I then headed off to a quiet corner of the hospital to get away from it all.

Of course, this sent my mum into a blind panic. She didn't know where I'd gone, so she rang my dad who came rushing over to the hospital. When he got there they found me sitting in a corridor and we had a huge row.

When we headed home my father lost his temper completely. All the emotions he'd been keeping pent up inside him came bursting out. I saw an anger in his eyes that I had never seen before.

At that moment I made my mind up.

My dad spent the night stomping around the house shouting at the top of his voice. 'Get on the phone, she's not having that baby,' he said at one point to my Heather. I had no idea who he wanted her to ring.

Looking back, I can understand why they were panicking. They thought I was throwing my life away. They had seen everything I was planning to do and, as far as they were concerned, I was now going to destroy my own future. As a parent myself, I can understand that. But at the time I didn't.

The next day I packed a little carrier bag of things, went into Enfield and drew out what money I had in my bank account. It wasn't very much, probably about £100, but it was enough to get a train to Colchester from Enfield and then to get a cab to the barracks where Tony was based.

I remember driving along the tree-lined road that led up to the barracks. The naïve girl in me was probably thinking that Tony was going to be standing there waiting to save me. The grown-up young woman knew he wouldn't.

I was pretty mature about the whole situation. I sensed that if I'd stayed at home my parents would probably have worn me down and persuaded me either to have an abortion or to let them adopt my child. I don't know what that would have done to me. I know I would never have got over it.

When I arrived at the barracks, Tony wasn't expecting me, of course. My dad had banned him from seeing me and we hadn't spoken for a week or two. But when he got over the shock of finding me on the camp he asked for some leave so we could sort things out.

It wasn't ever going to be as simple as me running into his arms and us living happily ever after, of course. Tony knew he was going to be posted to Germany quite soon. Members of the Army weren't allowed to take girlfriends with them, only wives, so there was no way I could go with him at the time. We were already talking about getting married by this stage, although we knew that I was too young to walk down the aisle legally without my father's permission. Getting his permission might be a bit of a problem, I guessed.

For now, our most immediate problem was finding me a home while I waited to have the baby. Fortunately Tony's family felt very differently to mine about my being pregnant. They were quite excited about the prospect, so when Tony called them they agreed to take me in up in Yorkshire.

I had been there once before, during the previous Christmas, although the memory of the visit still made me blush with embarrassment. The culture shock had been huge for me.

Back then, I came from what was Maggie Thatcher's London. I lived in a three-storey Victorian house in Enfield. When we arrived in Pontefract, Tony's hometown, we drove past a housing estate with smoke coming out of the chimneys, something I had never seen before. On the walls there was graffiti everywhere. There was a giant 'SCAB' daubed in red paint on a wall from the miners' strike. It looked really dingy.

'Can you imagine having to live there?' I said to Tony.

He didn't say a word.

We drove down into the village where Tony bought his mum, Zena, some chocolates then we turned around and drove back up the hill and on to that estate.

Talk about putting your foot in it. Tony told his parents

what I'd said. He thought it was funny, but his family didn't. To them I was from another world. I lived in London where I had a job working in accounts. I lived in a big family house. To them I was a posh southerner.

To be honest, I didn't get on particularly well with Zena. We never saw eye to eye, really. When Tony headed off to his new posting in Germany leaving me alone with her, life turned into a bit of a nightmare.

Because I was pregnant I was sick all the time. And I couldn't eat the food they cooked because of the way they cooked it. It sounds mad, but I was a London girl who liked her chips cooked in fat, not dripping. I couldn't eat the onion gravy. I would try to eat my dinner but I would throw up.

I lost a lot of weight because I wasn't eating. When I began my pregnancy I weighed 9 stone 4 lbs. Four or five months into the pregnancy, I weighed just 8 stone 3 lbs. I remember one day calling Tony from a phone box and passing out because I'd lost so much weight. When I came to, I was surprised that the baby survived. One of the relatives had come to pick me up.

Things came to a head with Zena when, after a few drinks one night, she told me she didn't want me living with her any more. Luckily Tony's grandmother Ivy, who lived not far away in Featherstone, agreed to take me in and I lived with her from September to November 1986, the last three months of my pregnancy.

She was great – she looked after me even though I didn't really know her and she didn't know me. It was Ivy who fed me up and got my weight back to where it should have been. Her home cooking was lovely, although she did commit the cardinal crime of introducing me to Galaxy chocolate.

She also taught me to knit. She had this knitting machine which she showed me how to operate and together we spent hours making baby clothes.

It was Ivy who really encouraged me to push on with our plans to get married. 'You and Tony will never be together in Germany unless you tie the knot,' she said.

I summoned up some courage and wrote to my dad, asking for permission. He refused, of course. I responded in typical fashion – I took him to court.

Looking back I can see how awful it must have been. I was eight months pregnant. I was going to be eighteen in January so if I hadn't been able to get married in October it wouldn't have mattered. We could have waited a few months. It wasn't as if I was going to be on the street.

But I was really headstrong and was determined to be Tony's wife before I became the mother of his child. So I took my poor dad to court so I could get married.

We turned up at the local Magistrates' Court on a Monday morning. It's amazing the effect a courthouse has on you, no matter what the reason for your appearance there. There were other people due up before the magistrates: shoplifters and people on GBH charges, all sorts. As I sat there waiting for our case to be heard I felt like a criminal.

Deep down I couldn't understand why I was having to go through this. I understood the law but I didn't see why I had to go to a courtroom like a petty villain. The anger that was building inside me would only grow worse as the morning wore on.

Tony and I were representing ourselves. We'd been told we didn't need a solicitor to put our case for us. My father, however, had engaged someone to represent him. We were told that he was on his way up from London. Unfortunately, he'd been delayed which meant that the case had been put back until later in the morning.

As we sat there waiting for the solicitor to show up, things just got more and more tense. The atmosphere was awful. I was eight months pregnant and life was stressful enough. I didn't need the extra anxiety. The courtrooms were separated from the entrance to the building by a set of electric doors. Every now and again they would make a noise and open up. Every time they did so I expected to see my dad walking through them.

Deep down I knew he wouldn't, of course. He had other children and a business to run and there I was in Yorkshire – which wasn't exactly around the corner. I would probably have done exactly the same thing and left me to it.

By mid-morning we were getting seriously worried that the case would be postponed. The clerk of the court had already asked us whether we could come back another day but we'd said no. Tony had to go to Germany at the weekend and we were hoping to arrange a wedding, we told him. Before the conversation got any further, my father's solicitor appeared. Within minutes we were being ushered into the courtroom.

By an amazing stroke of luck, one of the magistrates was an ex-Royal Signals officer. So the minute he knew who my husband-to-be was we got brownie points. That was the good news. The bad news was that my father's solicitor had been briefed to discredit and demean me in front of the magistrates.

I wasn't asked to give evidence, because of my age. Instead Tony took to the witness box. The solicitor got straight to the point. 'How do you know this baby is yours?' he asked him.

I sat there seething. 'How dare you say that?' I thought. I really couldn't understand how my father could allow someone to say that about me. I wasn't that kind of girl at all. And he knew it.

Tony gave a good account of himself, which obviously went down well with the magistrate. He explained the Army's rules on wives and girlfriends, and how he was being posted to Germany. He told the court that he wanted his newborn child and its mother with him as he served his country. The ex-Royal Signalman loved that and nodded sympathetically after Tony had finished.

The hearing only lasted a few minutes. At the end the magistrates gave us permission to get married. My father's solicitor didn't look too chuffed. He faced a long, miserable drive back down the M1.

As we left the courthouse I felt a mixture of emotions. I felt pleased that we could go ahead and get married. But I felt disgusted with my father and my family back in London for having done what they did in court. I swore I would have nothing more to do with them.

We had set the wedding for that Friday so I spent the next few days frantically preparing for what should have been the happiest day of my life. It didn't work out that way....

I didn't think it was quite right for me to wear white, so I bought a lovely aqua-green dress. I ordered some nice bouquets of flowers at the local florist and Tony organised a vintage car to take me to Pontefract Register Office, where the wedding ceremony was going to take place. An uncle of his, Les, apparently had a nice, old white car, he told me.

Ivy was great, as usual, and had made the wedding cake, a nice two-tiered fruitcake.

The week whizzed by and it was soon Friday, the wedding day. From the off, things didn't go quite the way I'd imagined they would.

Tony's uncle Les turned up in his vintage white car an hour before the ceremony. It turned out to be an MG Midget. I was eight months pregnant with this bowling ball of a stomach sticking out in front of me. Squeezing myself down into the low sporting seat was a challenge. And sitting there as Les bounced us along the roads was awful. It was like being in a bath.

Les was from Wakefield and didn't know his way around Pontefract at all. We ended up in the middle of the town with the Register Office in front of us, on the other side of the town's main square. The only problem was that it was market day and so the square was filled with stalls and closed to traffic. Les ended up driving across the pedestrianised area, dodging the markets stalls as we went. I was laughing all the way, which helped get rid of my nerves, I must say.

We had invited only about a dozen people. Tony's family, his mum and dad and brothers and aunts and uncles were there. We'd also invited a neighbour who I got on with quite well. There was absolutely nobody from my family.

It's fair to say, it wasn't the fairytale wedding of the year.

Looking back, what's also sad is that it wasn't a true reflection of Tony or of our relationship. We had wanted to get married, but at our own speed. Instead, we were being forced to get married now simply so we could go to Germany.

The wedding reception was held at an aunt's house. We stayed with Tony's Auntie Yvonne in Wakefield on the Friday night then headed back to Ivy's on the Saturday. We had a wedding night but not a honeymoon. At 2 a.m. on the Sunday morning Tony returned to camp, and then went on to Germany.

Tony rang me on the Sunday night to tell me he'd got there safely. He told me that he was going off on exercises the next day and he would be coming home in a fortnight's time after the exercises were over. 'I'll be home for when you have the baby,' he told me.

I didn't say anything to him but I knew that he wouldn't. I don't know if it was my being psychic or simply a strong maternal instinct, but I knew my baby was coming soon.

A week or so later I knew the time had arrived.

I remember going to bed and having a little chat with James inside my tummy. I had named him James all the way through, even though I didn't know he was a boy. Looking back, I think that was just a mother's instinct.

James was a name that had meaning in both our families. My Pops was called James, I had a favourite Uncle Jim and it was also my brother's middle name. It was a name within Tony's family as well. The first recorded Bennett in 1870 was James Bennett.

That night, I remember saying goodnight to James and thinking, 'See you tomorrow.'

The following day my waters broke and I was taken into Pontefract Hospital. Ivy was with me all the time. I don't know what I'd have done without her. I gave birth to a beautiful baby, a boy, as I had predicted. I was elated. If I'm honest, I'd been petrified that I would have a girl. I didn't want a daughter because I didn't want to recreate me. I didn't want the risk of me turning into my mother. So when I had James I thanked God my baby was a boy. I loved him more than I'd ever loved anything before in my life.

We weren't in hospital for long. James was born on the Monday and I discharged myself on the Wednesday. The next day, Thursday, I got myself a one-year passport. On the Friday, with my new baby in my arms, I headed to Germany, ready to settle into the life of an Army wife.

The feelings I had when I became a teenage mother have frequently proven useful in my mediumship, never more so than when I did a reading for a young woman. She'd arrived without an appointment, just before 5 p.m., when I was about to close the centre where I was working at the time. Ordinarily I would have told her to come back another time but I could tell by looking at her that she was in a bit of a state. So I agreed to read for her.

I normally ask people how old they are before doing a reading. As I've mentioned, I don't generally do readings for people under eighteen. She looked nineteen or twenty.

As soon as I sat down I knew she was pregnant. I could feel it. I felt nauseous and heavy, all the things I'd felt when

I was expecting. 'You're here because you're pregnant,' I said.

'How do you know that?' she asked, a bit taken aback. 'Nobody knows that.' Rather than becoming more tense, however, she relaxed. It was as if she was relieved to be sharing the burden of this secret.

I got some Tarot cards out and started doing a reading. I saw that she was not in a solid relationship. I could also see that she was terrified of telling her father she was pregnant. I sensed that history was repeating itself here. Her mother had been only sixteen when she'd had her. I could see that her mother had always told her that she felt her life was over when she got pregnant so young. She had kept warning her not to make the same mistake.

She just sat there, nodding at everything I was saying. 'Yes, that's right,' she kept repeating. 'How do you know all this?'

At this point I didn't tell her it was because I'd been through it myself. Instead of a normal reading, it turned into something of a counselling session. This girl was all over the place emotionally. But I felt myself able to guide her. What was funny about it was that I could see things from both sides. By that time I was a mother myself. So I could see the parents' perspective. But I could also see things from this young woman's point of view. I had been like her. I had been scared of my father, scared of repeating my mother's problems. I'd also had no-one to talk to about all this. I was determined that she would have someone to talk to – at least today. She needed someone to sit there and to understand what she was going through.

There was no question that she was going to keep the baby, which was again an echo of what had happened to me.

I told her that it wouldn't be the end of her life, far from it. She would still have opportunities in life. She would still have a future.

I told her about what had happened to me. 'I was seventeen when it happened to me,' I told her.

'So am I,' she said. She explained that she had been thinking of running away to have the baby, but by the end of the session I'd persuaded her to stay and face the music. I told her that her family would scream and shout a lot at first, but that eventually they'd support her. And so they did.

She came back to see me a few months later, with her new baby boy. She also had her mother with her, who looked like the proudest grandmother in the world.

Again it was an example of my life serving my mediumship. If I hadn't been through my own experience as a teenager, I'd never have been able to give that girl such sound advice. I believe every aspect of my life has been for a purpose. Here was yet more proof of it.

Tony was based with the Royal Signals at Celle, not far from Hanover in northern Germany. We had a huge flat on the outskirts of the town.

I was determined to make my marriage work and everything actually fell into place very nicely. I was very much an Army wife. The old saying that 'wives come after the men's boots' held true. When you're in an Army environment your husband is always more important than you, or at least that's the way it was then. This meant that Tony and I would see each other only at the weekends, which was the way it had always been back in England, so we didn't overwhelm each other. During the week Tony would go to work, which he took very seriously, and I would be at home with James, which I absolutely loved.

Caring for James was the most rewarding thing I'd done in my life so far. There were other mothers around on the camp and I spent a lot of time with them. There was a real community atmosphere. At the weekends we would go off shopping into the nearby town of Hohne, which had a really good choice of shops.

For the first few months of my married life I was really happy. The only thing that was missing was my family back in London. Motherhood had not only calmed me down a lot, it had also reminded me of how much I'd loved the good times we'd had as a family when I was growing up, at least during the early years before my parents split up. My only regret about being in Germany was that James didn't have that in his life. He didn't know his grandfather, in particular. That broke my heart.

Eventually it was me who broke the ice, for a change. After about nine months, I got in contact with Auntie Pauline, who, along with my nan, I had remained in contact with since coming to Germany.

I learned that my dad and Heather had moved to Hoddesdon, apparently. Pauline had their new number so I phoned the house. My brother answered. At first I thought it was my dad, his voice sounded so like his – that's how much he'd grown up since I'd last seen him. The call was very emotional for me. I cried over the phone.

'Why don't you come round,' Terence said, as if I was living around the corner. He was still only fifteen, and still at school.

I sensed the time was right to heal the wounds. 'OK,' I said.

So when James was nine months old we travelled home from Germany and I introduced him to my dad.

I knew we had to ease our way back into our relationship, that I couldn't just breeze back in there as if the events of a year or so earlier hadn't happened. So James and I stayed with Auntie Pauline. She helped a lot in rebuilding the bridges, I must say.

The house my dad and the family had moved to was lovely. It was a big bungalow by the river. My dad had pigeon lofts out the back, of course.

When I arrived the first person I saw was Terence. I gave my little brother a big cuddle. When my dad appeared I just fell into his arms. That's the way we were together, the way we still are. If we haven't seen each other for a while, we just give each other a big hug, say we love each other and that's it – back on track.

I was so happy but I was even happier when James took to his grandfather straight away. Within minutes the two of them were heading off to the pigeon lofts. My dad has that kind of energy about him. It was quite strange, as if we hadn't been away.

My mum Heather was beside herself with joy, I could tell. She was so relieved for my dad. She'd been through all that emotion with him. It had been hard for him not to have me around. She'd had to watch him suffer as if he'd been grieving.

It could, of course, have been very different. After all that had happened, they could have made it very hard for us to return but they didn't – quite the opposite. They made it very easy for us. The wounds were healed fairly easily, really. And I was so relieved to have my dad, mum and family back. After that, we were in touch all the time, as if there had never been a cross word exchanged. Well, almost.

I travelled back to Germany with a huge smile on my face. I was so pleased the rift had been healed. I wasn't smiling for long, however.

I had been having stomach pains for a few months. They would come and go and I'd assumed they were some sort of post-natal thing. They weren't so bad that I felt I needed to go to the doctor. A few aspirin normally did the trick.

But then one day back in Celle I felt the pains coming on again, more severely this time. Before I knew it I'd passed out. Luckily someone raised the alarm and I was taken to the barracks doctor. I knew there was something wrong but I had no idea what. My biggest concern was James, although I knew the other wives would make sure he was well looked after.

They did some tests on me and discovered I had polycystic ovaries, a condition which produces cysts in the ovaries. It's something that can vary a lot in seriousness. In the very worst cases a hysterectomy is the only treatment. In my case the doctors said it could be treated with an operation. But it was a major operation and required me to have a Caesarean-like incision made.

The few days that I spent in the camp hospital were

among the loneliest of my life. Tony was only able to come in to see me very briefly because of his duties.

There was another girl in there with me, the daughter of an officer. She was the same age as me, eighteen. She would lie in her bed screaming and shouting for her mummy and daddy. I remember thinking 'I'm your age'. I was suddenly reminded that I was still really only a child.

Typically, the surgeon who was going to operate on me only came to see me when Tony was there. It was Tony who had to give permission for the operation, not me. 'Let me explain what the situation is and what we need to do during the operation,' I heard the surgeon say. It felt very demeaning but I bit my tongue.

The operation went well. Afterwards they told me, through Tony, that they had removed a cyst the size of a lemon. I had obviously been ignoring it for months.

They also had to take part of an ovary away. As a result, they thought it was highly unlikely I would be able to have any more children. I certainly couldn't try and get pregnant again for the next two years. If I did I could cause myself serious problems.

We spent the first two years of our marriage in Germany but then Tony got posted to Northern Ireland, to Londonderry. The base was outside Londonderry in a small village called Limavady. It was 1990 and things were still very volatile with the Troubles.

We were always on the alert, even me and baby James. One of the saddest things I ever saw was when James was playing one day with a little electric Jaguar car that Tony's mum and dad had bought him. He was 'cleaning' his car just like his daddy did. I watched as he looked underneath his car. 'What are you doing, James?' I asked him.

'I'm checking my car for bombs,' he said. He was a two-year-old little boy. I hated the whole situation. This wasn't the kind of thing you want your two-year-old to be doing.

After a while Tony was promoted. He became a sergeant and we moved to the camp in Londonderry itself. It was then that we decided to try for a second child.

It was now almost four years since I'd had the cystectomy. I'd had regular check-ups and we'd talked to the doctors about the situation. They had been very non-committal. They'd explained there were now drugs that could help control the problem, but they said that they couldn't predict how I'd react to another pregnancy. It might be OK, it might not be. Effectively, they said it was up to us. So we decided to give it a try.

I got pregnant straight away. I was twenty-one by now, a lot more mature than I'd been when I'd been pregnant with James. I coped with the physical side of the pregnancy surprisingly well. I was very lucky that the standard of care in the hospitals in Northern Ireland was very high. Unlike in England, where I had been given only two scans during my pregnancy, I was given a scan every month. As well as making sure the baby was OK, the medical staff monitored me carefully too. It made the process much more relaxed than my first pregnancy, with all its dramas.

My biggest worry was the Troubles and the security situation in Londonderry. We still had to check the car for bombs every day, something which became quite a challenge when I got into the final months of my pregnancy. I could get down easily enough but getting back up was difficult.

Travelling around Londonderry was always quite a nerve-wracking experience. On the way into the city centre, there was one 'red area' that we passed through where we were told we must never stop under any circumstances. I would never take James into the city when I went shopping, and I was very careful when I was out with him. Socially, none of us ventured beyond the camp or the facilities that were laid on for us by the Army. The risks were too great.

Most worrying of all though were the incidents that happened on a daily basis.

One day I was standing outside the little centre where James went to play group. It was across the road from where we lived, inside an Army compound that was guarded by a watchtower. A lot of the wives were there and we were chatting away as normal while we waited for the children to be let out at 12 noon. It was a beautiful sunny day, I remember.

At 11.55 a.m. we heard two huge bombs going off in the city centre two miles away. When I looked in the direction the sound had come from I saw a giant plume of smoke slowly rising up into the air. It was as if all the sound in the world had been turned off. No-one screamed or shouted. Everyone just went silent. I know we were all thinking the same thing: has one of these children just lost their father?

What was really telling about it was the way that five minutes later the kids came out and everyone carried on as normal. Nobody talked about what we had just experienced. It was surreal. But that's the way we lived our lives over there.

I had promised my parents that I would come back home if I ever felt my life was in danger. But the truth was it was in danger all the time, so I hadn't thought about returning. I only came close to telling Tony I was leaving once and it happened not long after those bombs went off.

One night we were woken up in the small hours by a loud explosion. It was always hard to work out how far away these things had happened. But this one sounded pretty close. It was also obvious that people had died as a result of it going off.

The next morning, as the wives gathered at school we learned that there had been an attack on one of the checkpoints not far from the camp. An innocent local man had had explosives strapped to his chest and been forced to drive his car into the checkpoint. He and two soldiers had been killed instantly.

It was the details behind the story that stopped me in my tracks and made me wonder whether I should be living here. One of the soldiers killed was the husband of a mother I knew from the crèche where James spent time. She was a nice woman, great with the kids. Her husband had spoken to her at 4.30 a.m. that morning. When he'd hung up he'd told her he loved her. Five minutes later he'd been standing at the checkpoint when the car bomber arrived.

As it happened, Tony wasn't required to do checkpoint duties. But he could easily have been going through the checkpoint at that time. The other victim was an eighteen-year-old soldier. He hadn't been in Northern Ireland very long. It was his first night on sentry duty. They had only been able to identify him from the foot that had been left in his boot.

I didn't know it then, but I was going through experiences like this for a reason. Twenty or so years on from that day, while I was on stage at a theatre in the southwest, I connected with a young boy who had passed while serving in Iraq. He was just eighteen when he was killed in action.

I find it quite natural to get into the emotions of serving soldiers. When I was in Northern Ireland, I saw a lot of the single guys and how hard it was for them. The suicide rates among single men were high. As I connected with this soldier I got that feeling of isolation and fear that I'd experienced there.

I was able to use it to bring him through to his mother, who was in the audience. It was quite an intense connection for a couple of reasons. Firstly, the moment I felt his presence, I was immediately reminded of the eighteen-year-old who had died at his first checkpoint duty in Londonderry. I remembered how hard it had hit all of us who lived on the camp there. I had never forgotten him.

As I felt this boy's presence I saw that he too had been on his first tour of duty. 'He was seventeen when he joined, but he wasn't able to enter a theatre of combat until he was eighteen,' I said.

'Yes,' his mother confirmed.

I then began to see something else that I recognised. I saw him as an Army Cadet, spending time in camps, practising on rifle ranges. All my own memories of being in the Cadets came back to me. I saw that this boy had wanted to be a soldier since he was a kid. 'He had always wanted to be a soldier,' I said.

'Yes, that's right. Since he was a little boy,' his mother replied.

Sometimes, when I feel a spirit drawing really close to me, my energy levels go through the roof. I began to feel that way: as if he was coming up to me, as if to whisper in my ear. I felt a quite intense sense of emotions from him and then I heard him say: 'It was all I wanted to do.'

As a medium, I believe if you've fulfilled your dream you're free to leave this life.

His message to his mother was that, yes, it was heartbreaking that he was dead but she needed to know that he had fulfilled his dream in his lifetime. His mother was in tears, understandably. As a mother, I could feel her pain: it was almost unbearable. If I'd had a magic wand I would have brought him back for her. But I didn't.

But at least I was able to let her know that he was at peace and that he had died doing the one thing he had always wanted to do. He had lived his dream.

Again, if I hadn't been in the Cadets as a girl and then spent time in Northern Ireland I would not have known how to communicate his message as effectively as I think I did.

In January 1992 I developed a kidney problem and had to spend ten days in hospital. It's something that lots of expectant mothers go through; however, I'm not sure how many mums go through what I experienced a few weeks later when I went into labour. I gave birth with an armed guard watching over me.

I was booked into the Altnagelvin Hospital in Londonderry, where they'd been monitoring me all the way through my pregnancy. Getting to the hospital was a drama in itself. We needed a guard because we were going into Derry. The guard was for Tony not for me, of course.

I went to the hospital in an ambulance. It was a civilian ambulance so it wasn't allowed on the camp. I had to go to the gate and then walk out to meet the medics. As I travelled on my own in the ambulance to the hospital, Tony and his armed guard made their way there in a car.

I got to the hospital and was put in a delivery room. For the next few hours I paced up and down with two armed soldiers playing cards outside the door. Not your average experience of childbirth.

Given all the trouble we could have had, the birth was relatively straightforward. I had another boy; we called him Ryan. Six months after Ryan was born we were posted to Blandford in Dorset, in the southwest of England. I can't say I was sad to see the back of Londonderry.

We all loved it in Dorset, except James who, for some reason, wouldn't go to his playgroup. It wasn't long before we were on the move again, though, this time to Catterick – back in Tony's home county of Yorkshire. He had received another promotion, becoming Yeoman of the Signals.

Some time after Ryan had been born, I began to sense that things weren't quite right between Tony and me. I began to see things, images in my mind. I know now that they were clairvoyant images, showing me events that were happening or going to happen. I didn't know that then, though. Back then I wasn't quite sure what to make of them.

The first inkling I got of what was going on was when I sensed that Tony wasn't telling me the truth about his whereabouts. This wasn't completely new. When we were in Northern Ireland I sometimes used to ask him where he'd been all day and he'd deliberately lie. He would say that he'd been in the office and I would know that wasn't true because of what I'd have seen in my head. 'That's funny because I saw you getting out of a helicopter in a field today,' I'd say, which would freak him out. But I hadn't worried about it back then. Then, although I knew he was lying, I also realised he was lying to protect me and James.

It was different when we got back to England. I sensed he was somehow lying to protect himself.

Something else was going on then too. I know now that it was the beginning of what you might call my psychic awakening. At the time I just thought a lot of weird things were going on in my head.

To begin with, I was having a lot of really odd dreams. I started dreaming about panthers, for instance. A panther would either be circling me or, if something else was going on in the dream, be standing alongside me. I had absolutely no idea where it was coming from. It was really bizarre.

It was also about then that I began to realise that I had a natural gift for clairvoyance. I discovered I had a gift for reading palms.

Back in London I'd gone out with a group of friends to Camden Town. For a bit of fun I'd visited a palm reader, a hippy-like lady. It was, I can see now, a very accurate reading. She immediately picked up on something that I had felt deep down but that I hadn't faced up to yet. 'Your marriage is going to be over soon,' she told me.

No-one else would have known it. I hadn't spoken to anyone about it. I had been married for ten years. I wasn't married to a bad man, far from it; Tony was a good man, a good provider and a caring dad. There was nothing horrible going on. It was just that I was growing out of the marriage. Somehow she had picked up on it. And she had picked up on me.

Over a drink with the girls after the reading, I suddenly announced that I could read palms myself. I still have no idea why I said it. It just came out of the blue. But, of course, the girls leapt on it and made me do a reading there and then.

We were all in a bar. The girl who was sitting next to me gave me her hand. I didn't even know her. She just happened to be sitting next to me. I looked at the lines in her hand and started making things up. At least that's what I thought I was doing. 'This line means that you were brought up by your grandmother, not your mother,' I said. I was laughing as I did this because I thought I was doing a spoof reading. The ideas were just coming from my head. But as I carried on with the reading I noticed that she was crying. It turned out to be true that her grandmother had brought her up; her parents were still alive but she was estranged from them, and had felt abandoned all her life. I knew how she felt, of course.

I kept apologising but she told me not to. 'This is the best thing that's ever happened to me,' she said.

My best friend Bonnie was there too. 'Go on then, read my hand,' she said, smiling.

'OK, let's see,' I started. 'You're going to have two children and you're going to live in the countryside. You're going to love living there,' I added, again relying purely on a stream of consciousness.

Bonnie just laughed out loud. She was an Enfield girl through and through. She was married to a lovely guy called Neil, but the idea of her living in the countryside was laughable. At least it was then. A couple of years later she moved away from the city. She had two children, my godchildren Benjamin and Charlotte. And she couldn't be any happier than she is living where she does.

When I went back to the camp I pretty much forgot about my own attempt at palm reading, although the fact I'd seen that this girl had been raised by her grandmother kept preying on my mind for a while. I was more concerned with what the lady had told me when she'd read my hand. I knew she had been telling the truth. Within two months I'd made the decision to leave Tony.

Back home with Tony, I found that the images and thoughts I was getting in my head were becoming stronger. I found myself reading his thoughts at times. He would think something and I would say it out loud. I assumed it was because we were married. If you've been with someone for years, and we'd been together quite a long time now, you know each other's thoughts. You know what they are going to say.

But this was different. I was tuning into thoughts that he wasn't going to share with me. I would say things such as: 'Who was that girl with the long dark hair that you were with?'

And he'd say, 'Who told you, who's been talking?'

'No-one, I saw you walking up the hill back to camp with her.'

He'd just shoot me a look as if to say 'stupid woman'.

At this point I still didn't really understand that I had a gift. I was seeing more and more evidence of it but, truth be told, I didn't know what it meant. What I did know, however, was that everything was pointing in the same direction.

My marriage to Tony had been deteriorating for years. Like so many other couples we'd stayed together because we were in the habit of being together, even though we weren't happy.

I certainly wasn't. He never made me feel special; he wasn't the most romantic man. He didn't 'do' birthdays or Christmas or Valentine's Day. By New Year's Eve 1995, I had decided I couldn't stay in the marriage any longer unless things changed – but nothing did.

My birthday came. Nothing. Valentine's Day came. Nothing. I decided that was it. I knew it was a huge decision to take, and for a while I put it off. Two things were holding me back: the boys and Tony's career.

My feelings about the boys were mixed. I didn't want James and Ryan to feel like I felt when I was the child of divorced parents. But at the same time I wanted them to experience more of life. I didn't want them growing up inside the Army bubble. I had always dreamed of them going to a normal school and having a normal life, not living behind a wire, which they did as Army children.

With Tony, my biggest worry was that I might ruin his career by leaving. I realise now that was the way I'd been conditioned to think. My life as an Army wife had brainwashed me. But I believed that by leaving him without a dutiful Army wife to have at his side at the regimental dinners and the other social events, I would be harming his chances of climbing even further up the Army career ladder.

It was a conversation that I had with the Regimental Sergeant Major that changed my mind. I was chatting to him one night when he'd had a few drinks. I told him how unhappy I was and to my surprise he was sympathetic. 'I don't know why you are with him,' he said to me.

'Because if I leave he wouldn't get any more promotions,' I said.

He just looked at me and said: 'He's not going any further than he has got now.'

That was the key; it changed my life. Within a couple of days I had left. It had been coming for years, but now it had happened. Straightaway, I knew it had been the right thing to do.

In the end I didn't leave Tony because he was unfaithful to me. To my knowledge he never was, although I did predict that he would have an affair with his best friend's wife. Sure enough, he ended up marrying her. And he was also seeing someone new within two weeks of my leaving him.

No, the reason I left him was that I couldn't see my life with him any more. From a psychic point of view, I know now that if I'm going to do something in the future I can see it in my mind. If I'm supposed to go on holiday I can see where I'm going to go. If it's not supposed to happen I can't see it.

I left Tony in July that year. James was eight and Ryan was four. I was really worried about the impact it might have on the boys, and I remember apologising to James. 'I'm sorry I've taken you away from your dad but don't worry – I'll make sure you get to see him,' I told him.

'Don't worry about it, Mummy. You smile every day now, and you didn't when you were with Daddy,' he replied.

Talk about out of the mouths of babes. It had taken a child to see it. The smiler that I'd been known as when I was young had returned. Literally within days of leaving him, I was changing.

Shortly after we split up, I went to a summer school run by the Open University. I had been on a couple of courses before, but now I wasn't wearing my wedding ring. One of the tutors picked up on it. 'I thought you were married,' he said.

'I'm going through a divorce,' I replied.

'It's hard, isn't it?' he said with a sympathetic smile. 'But it looks like you're coming out of it. How long has it been since you separated?'

'Two weeks,' I said.

He didn't know what to say.

I wasn't carrying any guilt and I wasn't feeling negative about it. I knew I had made the right decision.

Looking back I can see that Tony and I just weren't right for each other. He wasn't a very emotional man, which was perfect at the time we got married because I wasn't opening up emotionally then either. That had changed for me, however. I needed to open up emotionally. I've never regretted the decision, despite what has happened since.

4 | Discovering the Gift

A lot of mediums and psychics discover their abilities at a young age, often when they are very small children. Many talk about being able to see and communicate with the spirit world from as early as three or four years of age. For me it was different. My life as a psychic medium didn't begin until much later, when I was in my late twenties and early thirties, in fact.

It wasn't that I didn't have experiences before this time. I did, as I've already explained. From an early age I had been experiencing things that, looking back, I can now see were evidence of my being clairvoyant, psychic and mediumistic at an early age. But they didn't make any sense to me at the time, which wasn't that surprising given that my early life didn't make much sense to me either.

It was only after my marriage to Tony came to an end that the pieces of the jigsaw fell into place. As ever, with me, they didn't do so neatly. There was a lot of messiness involved.

When I first left Tony I went to live with my mum and dad for a while. They had never really warmed to him, so I don't think they were surprised by my arrival on their doorstep. They were delighted to have their two grandsons under their roof for a while.

But by September of that year I had got another place to live, thanks to my sister-in-law, who was a letting agent. I also managed to get some work, doing accounts and payrolls for local companies. I was twenty-six and a single mother, I needed the money.

I didn't go out much and I wasn't very interested in men at that point. So when one day in early 1997, my sister-in-law Nicola asked me if I wanted to go along with her to a psychic fair I said yes immediately. I'd become more and more fascinated by palm reading and had continued to do readings, mostly for fun. I'd also developed some kind of psychic ability.

I used it when I had a rare night out, socialising with my friends. Men would approach us, spinning us their chat-up lines. I'd take one look at the guy and say: 'Yeah, right, but you're married and you've got a little girl at home'. Or when someone had told us that he did a certain job I'd say: 'No you don't, you wash cars for a living.' I'd always be right.

I still didn't claim to understand what it all meant, if anything, so a psychic fair seemed like a good place to go to find out more.

It was an interesting event, and by far the most interesting person there was a Tarot reader called Kimh. I use the word 'person' deliberately here because I'm still not really sure whether Kimh was a man or a woman. She was dressed as a woman but definitely had the body of a man. She also had a man's hands and a very deep voice.

I'd heard a bit about Tarot but didn't really know too much. I decided to have a reading to learn more. Looking back on it now Kimh gave me the most absolutely amazing reading. It wasn't so much that she got things right, even though she did. For instance, she told me that I was studying with the Open University, which was true. At the time I was doing a foundation course in art and religion.

What impressed me most was more the certainty with which she talked about my future. She told me that I would be teaching adults and that a lot of people would want to come and learn from me. At this point I was thinking of becoming a schoolteacher, so for a few moments I imagined that's what she meant. But before I could think about that too much she was telling me something else. 'You're a psychic and a medium,' she said. 'People will come to learn how to become psychics and mediums too.'

This made no sense to me whatsoever. 'Why would adults come to me to learn things? What did I know?'

Kimh told me that I would be taking my work all over the country. She said she could see me in my car driving up and down the country, doing my job. I thought that didn't sound right; it all seemed too far-fetched.

All the same, I bought some Tarot cards for myself before I left the fair. I'd enjoyed playing around with palm reading. I thought this might provide some fun too. Back home I started to study them more closely. The cards came with a book, but I soon decided I didn't like it. It offended my independent streak. It was too controlling. So I learned to read Tarot my own way, by looking at the pictures. This seemed logical to me. Each card has something like seventy-eight meanings, so I figured that anyone was free to interpret them in any way they wanted.

I began to read them in my own, individual way. I read

them first for my family. We were all round at my mum and dad's house one Sunday when someone suggested I bring out my cards. It was just for fun so that they could see what I could do.

My brother Terence was there with his wife Jean. They had no children at the time and she was a businesswoman. So I turned to her first, saying, 'Let's have a look at this and see what it says'. When I spread out the cards the dominant pictures I could see related to babies. I could also see problems associated with those babies.

'You're going to have a baby and the baby is going to cause problems with your business,' I told her. 'I think you're going to have trouble with the woman who works for you when you have the baby.'

She smiled as if to say it was nonsense. Again, as with my best friend Bonnie, it would take a few years for the prediction to bear fruit, but bear fruit it did. Jean went on to have a son called Thomas, who arrived prematurely. While she was on maternity leave the lady she worked with started making lots of errors and in the end I was called in to help sort out her business until she and the baby were strong enough to cope.

Of course, I had no idea this was going to happen at this point. That day at my dad's house, as far as everyone was concerned we were just playing about with the cards. It wasn't long, however, before I realised that this wasn't a game.

I had begun working for a local builder, doing his accounts and wages. We got on well and I had talked to him about my interest in palm reading and, in particular, Tarot cards.

One day it was particularly quiet in the office and we were having a tea break. 'Go on, do a reading for me – get your Tarot cards out,' he said.

At that point I didn't realise the full potential of what the cards could reveal, so I just starting turning cards in the way that I'd taught myself to.

My boss was married to an Asian lady, with whom he had two lovely kids. But as I turned the cards over all I could see was this woman with long blonde hair. I wasn't seeing his wife at all. However, I could see him getting married again and having two more children, sons, with this blonde woman.

He had been in a very jolly mood when we started but when I told him this it freaked him out completely. His face turned an ashen white and he was trembling, I thought with anger. 'None of that's going to happen,' he growled, rising suddenly out of his chair.

Sometimes, nowadays when I walk past people I get almost electric shock-like 'flashes' of information. I experienced this for the first time as he walked past me on his way out of the room. Suddenly I got this flash of passport photos, which I sensed he had in his top pocket. I was annoyed that he had doubted what I'd told him so I just came out with what I'd seen. 'You've got the photos of the blonde woman in your top pocket,' I said.

Well, that just sent him storming out of the door as fast as his legs could carry him. I was worried that I'd really offended him. For the rest of the day I sat in the office, waiting for him to come in and give me my cards. Just before I was about to head home he re-appeared. He wasn't carrying my P45, but some photos.

They were the passport photos I'd seen in the flash. He confessed that, yes, he was having an affair with this woman. She was, like him, from the north of England. She was blonde and very attractive. He poured his heart out about how mixed up he was about being unfaithful to his wife. He swore me to secrecy, which, of course, he didn't need to do. I already knew I had to keep a lot of things to myself from now on.

As I headed home that evening I felt stunned. I was now convinced this really wasn't something to be taken lightly.

One morning a year or so later, in early 2000, I was sitting in the bedroom of my house in Hoddesdon getting ready for a normal, working day.

A lot had happened in the year since the psychic fair. One thing was that I'd started going out with a man called Simon. He'd moved in with the boys and me, and things were going well. That morning he had made me breakfast before heading off to work. I'd taken the boys to school, so I was in the house alone.

It was a normal, run-of-the-mill morning, but then, as I was brushing my hair, I began to hear a disconnected voice. I recognised it immediately. It was Simon's ex-partner, a lady I knew quite well. She was delivering a very clear message, over and over again: '*He's done it to me; he's going to do it to you.*'

I'd not really heard a voice like this since I'd got pregnant. I'd forgotten about them really, so I dismissed this one at first. I put it down to my overactive imagination. Besides, it didn't make sense. Who was she talking about and what had he done to her?

As the day wore on, however, I had more weird experiences. Half an hour or so after I had heard Simon's ex-partner talking to me I was leaving the house and heading off for work. I was thinking about the day ahead and the accounts work I had to finish that morning. I wasn't thinking about my relationship at all. But then suddenly and quite vividly I found myself thinking: 'I wonder what it's going to be like to be single again?'

I remember thinking how strange it was that this thought had just popped into my head like that. 'Where did that come from?' I asked myself. It was just like when I'd been walking up the hill with my 'friend' Joanne all those years ago. It was as if someone else was putting these thoughts into my mind. They were definitely not my thoughts.

Strange things like this continued happening throughout the day. At one point during the early afternoon I suddenly had a strong image of Simon driving down a motorway, heading away from where we lived together. I could see him quite clearly at the wheel of a car. Yet his drive to work took him nowhere near a motorway. 'Why is he on the motorway?' I asked myself.

As usual, I finished work around mid-afternoon so that I could be there when my sons got home from school. Normally I would have pulled up at the house and gone indoors to wait for them but today, for some reason, I didn't. Instead I drove straight on and headed to school to pick them up, where I found my cousin Sue.

'I had a very strange dream about you last night,' she said.

'What was that?' I asked.

'I came into your house and there was a note on your mantelpiece from Simon,' she said. 'It was like he was leaving you.'

'You're just having spooky dreams,' I laughed. As far as I was concerned our relationship was fine. We were both content and life was reasonably good. I thought I could spot if there were problems.

I asked Sue back to my house for a coffee. As we walked into the living room, we both froze. There on the mantelpiece was a piece of paper with Simon's handwriting on it. The scribbled note explained that he had packed his bags and left. Just like that. He said he had been unhappy and that he didn't think things would work out long term.

His leaving left me in a state of shock. It wasn't just the fact that he had ended our relationship so abruptly that upset me. It was the fact that I had been bombarded with all these thoughts and feelings which had been subconsciously telling me he was going to leave. And I hadn't listened to them.

I decided there and then that it was about time I really started understanding these abilities, whatever they might be.

I'm sure it wasn't a coincidence that, a week or so later, Sue rang me up asking me if I'd like to go to a psychic fair in nearby Harlow the following Sunday evening.

'Come on, it'll be fun,' she promised, 'and you could do with some fun.'

It had been a few years since I'd been to the fair where I met the strange Tarot reader Kimh. I expected a similar type of event. It was soon clear that it was a more serious affair.

The fair was being held in a large, circus-like tent. From the moment I stepped in, I began to experience a strange mixture of emotions.

A weird-looking man dressed in black was standing by the entrance. As I scanned the inside of the tent I also saw a man dressed like a Native American. According to the sign next to him his name was Tony Eagletree.

Oh, it's going to be all weirdoes in here, I thought to myself. 'They're all mad,' I whispered to Sue.

There was something about the atmosphere in the place that made me feel really sick and all out of balance. There was a huge stand with crystals. I had had no contact with crystals before. I know now that crystals have different properties. They can make you feel high or low. They have great healing properties and can be used for clairvoyant readings too. I also know that I'm really susceptible to their energy. But at the time all I could sense was that I was feeling distinctly sick.

These sensations only added to the discomfort I already felt inside the tent. Sue went off to have a reading from a strange-looking lady. There was no-one else around so I went over to see this Tony Eagletree character. He invited me to sit down for a reading.

'Why not?' I thought. 'I've got nothing to lose.'

To be honest, I just thought he was going to make something up. I really thought that he was a charlatan. Anyone with a name like that had to be, didn't he?

He told me he was going to read some special Native American cards. As he sat there shuffling the cards all I could think about was my love life.

'What can you tell me about what happened with Simon,' I was saying to myself. I didn't get any of that, however. He started talking about my children and my ex-husband. It was all accurate stuff but I wasn't really interested.

Then he said something that stopped me in my tracks. 'You've got a hole inside you that has never been filled,' he said.

'Hold on a minute,' I thought. 'You've got me there. That makes sense to me.'

As the reading continued he kept turning the cards over. Suddenly every picture he turned up was of a group of people sitting in a circle. 'You should be sitting in a circle,' he said.

'What's a circle?' I asked, genuinely not knowing what he meant.

'A mediumship circle. Where people get together to communicate with the spirit world,' he explained. He nodded across to another table. 'See that man over there in black? His name's Barry and he runs one.'

'OK,' I said hoping he would shut up about circles and carry on with my reading. 'I'll go over and talk to him later.' I had no intention of talking to Barry, of course. I intended to run out of the place. It was all beginning to freak me out.

As the reading went on Tony Eagletree started talking about my having a purpose and a future. 'Lots of people will come to you for help and for guidance,' he said. This was a little bit like what I'd heard from Kimh. Again I guessed it was something to do with my studies with the Open University. What else could it mean?

I really wasn't taking what he was saying very seriously at all, which must have been obvious because he then got cross with me. 'You're not listening to anything they're telling you, are you?' he snapped.

'What? Who is telling me? Who are they?'

'The spirit world.'

'I really have got a nutter here,' I thought. I didn't know

anything about this stuff at all. I knew nothing about mediumship. To be honest at that point in my life I didn't believe you could talk to the spirit world, which is very odd considering what I'm doing now.

Tony was clearly determined to persuade me differently, however, and carried on with the reading. It was then that he began to tell me things that he had no right to know. First he said he had my grandfather, my dad's father, with him and went on to describe him to an absolute tee. He then described a woman, who I didn't know, and told me she was my grandmother.

'She's alive and living in London,' I said.

'No, this one's from Ireland,' he insisted.

'Oh. That would be my mother's family. I don't know them. I've never met her, so why would she want to come and talk to me?' I wondered, mildly annoyed.

'She's passed over into the spirit world and her purpose isn't to repair everything that has happened to you, but she is going to make your life better.'

It was then that he told me something that left me stunned. 'I've got your grandad here now. He is telling me he had a heart attack when you were fourteen,' he said.

'Yes,' I said, hesitantly.

'You were in the bath at the time and have a scar to remind you of it.'

Well that just about did it. There was no way in the world that anyone else would have known that. One night, when I was fourteen, I was in the bath upstairs in our house in Enfield. I was shaving my legs in the bath and, being naughty, I was doing it quickly with my dad's razor, hoping that no-one would catch me.

My grandad, Stanley, was visiting us at the time. Suddenly I heard my brother Terence shouting at the top of his voice. 'Help, help, grandad's having a heart attack!' In a state of shock I had cut right into my ankle with the razor. There had been blood everywhere. I've still got the scar.

It's fair to say that after that observation Tony Eagletree had my complete attention.

'So, are you going to speak to Barry over there about your gift?' he asked me.

By now I was somewhat shaken. 'OK,' I nodded. 'I think perhaps I better had.'

By that point he had scared me and I was feeling a bit sick. I didn't know what the hell was going on. My cousin Sue's reading had finished by now and she came to find me, but I was so thrown by what had happened with this Tony Eagletree character that I went over to talk to Barry.

'Tony over there says I should come to your circle,' I said.

'Well, it's about time,' he smiled.

'What do you mean?'

Now it was Barry's turn to start telling me things about myself. 'You've been told this before and you've ignored it,' he said. I thought back to Kimh and the palm reader in Camden. This must have been what they were talking about when they mentioned teaching. He continued: 'The circle sits on Wednesday night in the Latton Bush Centre in Harlow. It costs £2.50. I'll see you there.'

I was so overwhelmed by the reception I'd got at the fair that I knew I had to go along to the circle. I still wasn't one hundred per cent sure I trusted these people. It sounds crazy now, but I thought they might even slip me some kind of hallucinogenic and make me strip naked. So I asked Sue to come along with me, for morale and any other kind of support I might need.

We both thought it was going to be a fun evening, regardless. We'd met so many odd characters at the fair; we were laughing all the way there, wondering who we'd find waiting for us this time. To be honest, I had every intention of going there just the once, coming home and never returning ever again. I just wanted to make more sense of what I'd been told.

When we got to the Latton Bush Centre we were directed to a room inside the building. As we walked along the corridor towards it, I told Sue that she had to sit next to me – that we couldn't be separated that evening. 'If they offer you water don't drink it. It could be spiked with hallucinogenic drugs,' I said, deadly seriously. 'And don't agree to change your clothes; they might just be trying to get us naked.'

When we reached the room where the circle was meeting we realised the door was wide open. Whoever was waiting inside could easily have listened to our entire conversation. As we walked in and looked at the people sitting quietly in a ring of chairs, there was no doubt from the looks on their faces that they'd heard every word we'd said. I wanted the ground to open up and swallow me.

Fortunately Barry stepped forward, laughing. 'Hello, glad you could come. Just sit yourselves down,' he said.

There was a real mixture of different types of people, a group of people that you would probably never see gathered together in the same place. There were some very educated people, people off the street, housewives and single mums, lawyers and policemen.

Also there was Barry's dad Gregory, who is now in the spirit world, and an odd-looking woman who was inviting me to sit next to her. I sat down and Sue sat in the row directly behind me.

I soon regretted my choice of seat. 'There's a wedding dress sitting alongside you that's just dropped to the floor – so that means you've recently come out of a relationship,' the woman observed.

Because we were new to the group, the circle decided they were going to begin by reading for us. They knew Sue and I were cousins even though we didn't really look alike. Barry said he felt a link to a grandad that we shared but that he was more attached to me than her, which was absolutely true. Sue wouldn't have disagreed with the fact that I was grandad's favourite.

As things progressed, I felt the same strange feeling I'd felt in the tent at the psychic fair on the previous Sunday. It was even more oppressive this time. I felt as if the whole room had been locked down. It was almost as if we had bars above us. They also had red lights in there so the room was very dim. I was soon feeling even more uneasy.

'So, tell me about the panther,' Barry said out of the blue. That really threw me. Since I'd first seen them, way back when I was still with Tony living in Blandford, the panthers had been an almost constant presence in my dreams. They'd been there in virtually every vivid dream I'd had, but I'd told no-one about them. How the hell did he know about them?

I was intrigued so I told him the truth. 'I see a panther in my dreams a lot,' I said. 'It's always hanging around me, watching me.'

'Yes. I know,' he said.

'So what does it mean?' I wanted to know, really not sure what to expect as an answer.

'It's a totem animal, an animal guide. It's helping to bring you forward,' Barry explained.

'Right…' I said. 'So why isn't it actually doing anything in the dreams?'

Barry grinned. 'It's a panther – it can't mix, can it? It wants to bring you forward but it has to hide in the shadows at the same time.' I really wasn't sure what to make of that. But the meeting wasn't just about me, of course, and Barry's comments sparked a conversation about spirit guides among the whole circle. I didn't know what they were talking about.

We were then all told to sit back, relax and let our guides come forward. I turned round and caught Sue's eye at this point. We both giggled. 'This is going to be fun,' I thought. But I was soon thinking rather differently. All of a sudden I felt as if I'd grown. I felt massive. My hands felt huge. That was strange enough, but then I felt I had stubble all over my face. I could also feel a woolly hat pulled over my head. I told myself to snap out of it. 'This is weird,' I said to myself. 'They've slipped me something.'

But then all I could see was an image of a man in my head. I also felt like I was being pushed around physically. I looked behind me to see whether there was anyone pushing me, but there wasn't anyone. No-one had moved.

Barry noticed and asked me to describe what I was feeling. I began describing some of the things I was experiencing, such as my size and the heightened energy level I was feeling. As I did so everyone in the room was nodding.

I deliberately didn't mention the feeling on my face. I thought everyone would think I was mad. It was Sue, my cousin, who was the first to say something. 'I can't go home with you looking like that,' she said.

'Like what?' I said.

'You look like a bloke.'

Everyone laughed. What she and everyone else could see was that I suddenly seemed to have a beard.

Barry then told me to go around everyone else in the room and explain what I felt when I looked at them. There was a guy sitting opposite me. I hadn't really noticed him there before. When I looked at him I got this strong sensation in my arm, as if someone was draining my blood. 'I feel like someone is taking my blood,' I said.

With that the guy undid his sleeves, rolled up his shirt and showed me the plaster he was still wearing from the blood tests he'd had done that day. I was gobsmacked.

It was one of the most exhilarating moments of my life. I was suddenly buzzing with the sense that I could feel these other people. To be honest, anything could have happened and I wouldn't have been surprised.

At that point I thought this was normal, that everyone who came along to a circle like this had this experience. I hadn't really sussed that no-one else was doing what I was doing.

It was Barry who spelled out what had happened. 'Tracy you have a gift, a special gift,' he said. He explained to me what the beard meant. 'You're a trance medium and that was your guide showing himself through transfiguration,' he said.

I had never heard of transfiguration. Ever. And what was a guide? I thought they were little girls in blue uniforms.

Barry continued, 'Tracy, I feel that you're going to be a very well known medium. You're going to be on television and you're going to stand on stage giving messages from the spirit world.' He went on: 'There will be books that will be written by you which will encourage people, but not in an old-fashioned way.'

He went on like that for a minute before he stopped.

I just looked at him and shook my head. 'You're mad, absolutely mad,' I said.

Sue and I laughed about it all the way home. Deep down, however, I knew that this really wasn't a laughing matter. As did Sue.

I knew that there was something to what Barry was saying. Too many strange things had happened that night – and over the previous weeks, months and years – for me not to suspect he was talking some sense. I clearly did have some kind of gift.

From that Wednesday on, I was hooked. It didn't matter what else was going on; I was there, sitting in that circle. I wanted to know more. I wanted to learn.

In time it would be different, but back then I wasn't doing it for anyone else. I was doing it for myself, for me. I needed to know what this gift was, and what I could do with it.

5 | Finding the Right Path

Suddenly I felt like I had a clear direction in my life again.

After what happened that night in Harlow, I was determined to learn about this gift that I had been told I had. I was still doing people's accounts, working at the builders and other local businesses. But I also decided I was going to take the leap and start doing paid Tarot readings. I knew I had some sort of talent. I'd read for lots of friends and family, developing my technique. And I'd never had any unhappy customers.

All I needed was premises where I could do readings.

Through the regular Wednesday night circle, I had met Graham, a healer who ran a centre called 'Charmed' in Cheshunt. He let various therapists, psychics and mediums use rooms there. I got on well with Graham and he agreed to let me do readings in one of his rooms. I stuck an advert up in the window and waited for a response. I was soon getting calls. I was chuffed when I got four bookings for the first day I was going to be there, a Saturday.

No sooner had I begun reading than I had to start learning the rules of my second profession. It was steep learning curve. I still read the cards instinctively, and built my own stories from the images that appeared. This was the method that had worked for me so far and, as the old saying goes, if it isn't broke don't fix it, so I stuck to it. Because I relied on my gut feelings so much I just came out with whatever was in my head most of the time. I just said the things that I felt.

However, I learned immediately that, as a professional Tarot reader, that wasn't always the best idea.

That Saturday was a big day for me. I was very excited.

My very first client, a lady, came in early that morning. She was quite tall, a housewife. You could tell she was a mum with kids. She had very short, unstylish hair and was in her late 30s early 40s.

I started laying out my cards in my usual way, reading them in my own style. I talked to her about her children. She was anxious about her daughter being able to get into a secondary school and I was able to put her mind at rest that it was going to be OK. I talked to her about the house and it was all OK again. I talked about her and it was all OK.

But then, when I started talking about her husband, it just didn't feel right.

To me Tarot cards don't have a set meaning. I know what they mean to me. Each time I read them, a story comes out of the cards, which means something. In this reading, I saw that there were two women and a man in the middle spread of cards that I'd laid out. To me, that meant that her husband had another woman in his life.

I was still excited at my ability to read the cards and before I'd really thought about it I'd blurted out what I was seeing: 'Your husband is having an affair!'

The lady looked stunned for a second. 'No, he isn't,' she said crossly.

I was so enthusiastic about what I was doing that I decided to explain to her what I'd seen. Every time I turned the cards I saw the three of them.

'This isn't a prediction – this is happening now,' I persevered. 'Your husband is having an affair with a woman who smiles at you every day. It's almost as if he is having an affair with your best friend.'

'Impossible,' she said, looking quite hurt by now. 'My husband hasn't got it in him. I'm not happy with that.'

I sensed that she was uncomfortable with the way the reading was going so I decided to end it there. I even offered her money back but she didn't want it.

'I came to make sure my children are going to be all right,' she said. 'And you told me they are, so that's OK.'

'I'm sorry; maybe I've misinterpreted it,' I said trying to calm. It wasn't the best of starts to my first day, I thought.

I didn't have too long to dwell on what had happened because my second client was already waiting for her hour-long session. That went fine, without any major revelations like the first one.

After that lady left, I welcomed in my third client of the morning. She was quite a glamorous lady. She had long black hair and looked like she had come straight from the hairdressers. She was very confident, very feminine, quite a bouncy, bubbly character.

I began the reading, talking about her children and her husband. And then I started reading about the other man in her life. Again the signs were unmistakable. When I started looking at the spread in more detail I found the exact same cards as the first woman. There were the three figures – this time two men and a woman – with the raunchy card in the middle.

Again, I just came out with it. 'You're having an affair – you naughty girl!' I said, laughing.

She just looked at me. She didn't say anything either way, which was confirmation enough to me that I was right. But I could see that she was getting annoyed with me. So again I said this wasn't a prediction but was happening now. 'It's going on now,' I explained. 'And I see it's very happy. There is a lot of laughter around it.'

It was at that point that I suddenly realised there was something not quite right here again. The first reading kept coming back into my head. To begin with I just thought it was something in the water – maybe everyone was having an affair at that moment! But then the lady started gesturing for me to stop working with the cards.

'I need to know what you told the first lady you saw today,' she said.

I was slightly taken aback by this. 'How did she know who had been in to see me?' I wondered. I said, 'Well, no sorry, I can't tell you. She was a private client and everything we talked about is confidential. As it is with you and me.' It was really awkward for a moment.

'I really need to know,' she insisted.

'Why do you need to know?'

'Because she's my best friend. When she was doing her reading with you she was looking after my children and now while I'm here she's looking after my children.'

They had both been booked in and they'd allowed a gap

of an hour between the two readings so they could hand over.

She must have seen something in my face because she then asked me straight out, 'Did you tell her that I'm having an affair with her husband?'

This really threw me. In my head all I could hear was 'I knew it, I knew it'. But I had to tell her that I couldn't divulge anything.

After that things turned even more surreal for a minute or two. She even started asking me for advice. 'So what am I going to do,' she said. 'Is he going to leave her? Tell me what's going to happen.'

At that point I stopped the reading, which probably confirmed to her that I did know what was going on. She left, looking distinctly worried. I could only imagine that she must have picked up on something in her friend's body language.

I wondered afterwards what happened to them but I never found out. Unsurprisingly neither of them came back to see me again.

Lots of other people did, however. And as they came to see me I learned more valuable lessons.

A few weeks later I did a reading for a guy I knew from around the town. He was a florist just up the road; a lovely old guy aged almost seventy-five. As I turned the cards over, a clear picture emerged quite quickly. It was obvious to me that he needed to get some treatment for his heart.

I'd learned not to go diving in with sweeping statements by now. 'You need a bit of an MOT,' I said with a smile.

He looked slightly alarmed, but I soon calmed him down. I didn't think he was going to die. 'The cards are showing me that you're going to have an operation, but that operation will give you a new lease of life. You'll come off the operating table and feel much better,' I explained.

I could see he was relieved – perhaps a little too relieved. I sensed that he was a typical man and when it came to his health he might stick his head in the sand, like an ostrich. 'But you must get to the doctors and sort it out; otherwise it'll be a different story,' I added, to make sure he'd have himself checked out.

'All right, I'll go, I promise,' he reassured me.

When we'd finished the reading he headed back to his florists shop, seemingly happy. But within a couple of hours he collapsed and had to be rushed to hospital in an ambulance.

When he came round he was told he needed a major heart operation and was asked to sign a consent form, which he did. He had the operation that afternoon, and by the following Monday, he was lying in bed, as chirpy as a teenager.

It was only the following Saturday that I discovered all this. I found out when his daughter arrived with a bouquet of flowers. 'You saved my father's life,' she said.

For once in my life, I was speechless.

She explained, 'He told me that you had said he needed an operation, but you had also told him that he was going to come out of it all right.'

'That's right,' I said.

'That was so important. We had been trying to get him to

go to the doctors for months but he wouldn't go because he was frightened of having an operation and dying.'

'Oh, OK,' I said cautiously.

'Because of what you told him he was happy to have the operation. He wouldn't have been otherwise. You told him he would be all right. So he went into it with a positive attitude.'

The bunch of flowers she gave me occupied pride of place at home for a couple of weeks. Whenever I looked at them I smiled inwardly. Whatever it was I was doing, it was creating some good.

I had a new vocation in life. And it felt wonderful.

By the spring of 2002, I was faced with a big decision.

I was still doing the accounts for my friend at the builders and living with the boys in Hoddesdon. But I was also getting more and more work as a Tarot reader. It seemed that I was able to use my gift to help people, and I wanted to develop that. I wanted to see where it might take me.

With this in mind, a few people had said to me that I should get some professional counselling skills. The University of Hertfordshire ran a good counselling course, but there was no way I could do it part time. I would have to become a full-time student.

The choice I had to make was hard: to carry on earning a steady income or to take a risk and become a student. I decided to take a leap of faith and sign up for the course.

I knew that money would be tight but, with the income I was now making from the Tarot readings, I reckoned I could do it. Of course, it wasn't quite that simple; things never were in my life.

A few weeks after I'd quit my job, I got a letter from my landlord. Somehow he had got wind of what I was doing. He spelled out that the tenancy was dependent upon my having a job. He'd correctly assumed I was going to have to rely on some benefits so that I could go and study. The letter said that as I would no longer be a professional tenant he didn't want me in his house.

And so it was that in May 2002 I was made homeless.

This didn't go down very well with my family, not least because I soon found out that it was my sister-in-law, the original letting agent, who had told my landlord about my change in circumstances. She was very professional about her job and she explained that knowing about my circumstances had put her in a difficult situation. I understood her predicament – eventually.

Losing the house left me at a crossroads in terms of the way I lived. I had to give my boys some security and stability in their lives. We'd been living in rented accommodation ever since I'd left Tony. The trouble with that was that we never knew when we might have to move on. It was always uncertain. The boys and I had moved five times in five years, and we had been on the move before that when we were an Army family. I didn't want them to think that this was the way life had to be.

I suppose I could have gone to my dad and asked him to help me with a mortgage to get a house. But I didn't want to do that. The answer, I decided, was to put ourselves up for a council flat.

There was a lot of red tape to go through, and we were

told we'd have to go on a waiting list; I was advised it would take a few months. In the meantime we were told that we'd have to live in a hostel.

My heart sank when I heard this. How had it come to this? But living in the hostel seemed like a necessary short-term step while we waited for the security that a council flat would give us. So I bit the bullet. Of course, really I was just exercising my independent streak again. Part of me wanted to get a secure, stable home for the boys and myself without anyone's help.

In theory it was a good move. But it didn't work out that way. At first it was fine. I know it sounds crazy, but we were kind of lucky. We were put in a house with a big room for a family downstairs and then two rooms for a family upstairs. There was also a bathroom upstairs and a shower room and a communal toilet downstairs. There was a communal kitchen too.

Our rooms were small, but we could survive there for a while. The boys had a small bedroom with bunk beds and a wardrobe. I had a slightly bigger room with a fridge freezer and a chest of drawers and a wardrobe.

When we moved in there was a man living on his own downstairs. But he soon moved out, to be replaced by a lady, Jane, who moved in with her children, two daughters and a son. There is a terrible stigma to hostels. You imagine they are full of all sorts of people, down and outs, people at the bottom of the social ladder. But luckily Jane and her children were lovely.

We agreed not to use each other's toilet, which was very important. We only shared the shower room. We also tried to use the kitchen at different times, so as to give ourselves as much time together as families. For a while life there was bearable.

A few things kept my spirits up during those early months. Jane's friendship was a great help, as was the patience and understanding the boys showed.

They never complained about living in the hostel, even though it must have been awful for the pair of them to be sharing a small, cramped bedroom. It was awkward when it came to their school friends too; we could hardly invite them back to the hostel for sleepovers or parties. But the boys put up with it all.

They were also really supportive of what I was doing with my readings, and I spoke openly to both of them about it. I had always been honest with them and from day one they were fine about it. In fact, they would sit up and wait for me to get back from circle nights, dying to find out what had happened. They totally understood the gift I had and encouraged me to use it, which was a great source of strength for me.

Graham's support at 'Charmed' and the people in the circle was crucial too.

On a personal level, I'd started a relationship with a childhood friend, Adam. We'd known each other since we were nine years old. I'd first met him one day while I was sitting on a swing in a park, waiting for my dad, who was at a pigeon club nearby. Adam had come over with a group of other boys and – as boys do – he'd asked me which one of them I wanted to be my boyfriend. I'd chosen him. I can remember looking at him and thinking 'I'm going to marry you one day.' Not my most accurate prediction, as it turned out.

I'd got in contact with him again via my sister Amanda. We'd hit it off straight away and had started seeing each other. Adam had a nice house not far away where I'd go and stay at the weekends. The boys would come too. It became our great escape from the hostel.

We'd only been seeing each other a few months but Adam was already hinting that I should go and live with him rather than stay at the hostel. In a sense, he was trying to save me. But I didn't want to be saved. I was determined to get me and the boys somewhere on our own. I was as stubborn as ever.

The only major downside to my new relationship was that Adam was completely sceptical about what I did. I didn't mind that he wasn't convinced initially. I've found over the years that men are much more difficult to convince when I'm practising mediumship. You have to provide them with a lot more convincing evidence than a woman generally needs. That's fine by me – in fact I welcome the challenge.

But Adam was so anti the whole thing that he could get angry if I ever said anything he considered to be out of the ordinary.

He was heavily into football and Manchester United. At one point there was a lot of fuss on the TV news and in the newspapers about David Beckham. 'I had a dream about him,' I said one weekend.

He looked at me as if to say: 'I bet you did!'

'No, not that kind of dream – I dreamt he was sitting in an American diner reading a foreign newspaper. It's not French or German, could be Spanish.'

Adam got really cross with me. 'That's not being psychic. That's you reading the newspapers saying he's going to leave Man United to join Real Madrid,' he said.

'He won't go there, I know he won't,' I said firmly. I wasn't into football at all, so I didn't know what Adam was talking about. I really couldn't care less where Beckham played football. I just knew what I'd seen in my dream.

Later that day we were in the car and the news came on the radio, announcing that Beckham was leaving Manchester United and moving to Spain to play for Real Madrid. The guy on the radio said that Beckham was in America when he made the announcement.

I didn't say a word. Nor did Adam.

Besides the support of friends and close family, another thing that got me through the nights at the hostel was watching videos of an American medium that Graham had introduced me to, a man called John Edward. I hadn't really seen that many mediums in action before. I hadn't been brought up through the spiritualist churches where most people first encounter mediums at work, so it was all quite new to me.

What I loved about John Edward was his honesty. If someone was being uncertain about whether a message was for them he would insist on it being one hundred per cent right or he wouldn't move on with them. I could imagine a lot of mediums wouldn't be so strict in their principles.

I also liked the fact that he didn't waffle. He spoke quickly and directly and got to the point of his messages. He seemed very modern, again in contrast to a lot of spiritualist mediums, who seemed almost to be from a bygone age at times.

What I liked most about him, however, was that he was being himself. He also seemed a normal person – like me really. The more I learned about him, the more I liked the sound of him. He had been raised by a single mother and had started by reading Tarot cards. His path sounded kind of similar to mine. He made me think that, if I ever did something with this gift of mine, I would do the same as he had done: I would always be me.

It was inevitable. After a few months stuck in the hostel, my spirits began to fade. Whenever I contacted the housing department about when we might be put into a council home they told me there was no news.

As planned I had enrolled at University and gone along to the classes in September and October. But they had been tougher than I'd imagined, not academically but emotionally. The counselling course involved my baring my soul to a group of strangers as part of the preparation work. I had to look at my life before I could look at the lives of others. I knew why I was doing it, but that didn't make it any easier. Sitting there, endlessly dissecting what had happened in my early life, brought back all sorts of painful memories for me, particularly about my mother.

So I was spending part of my days reliving the worst memories of my difficult childhood and then coming home to the hostel, where I was spending night after night on my own with the kids. This was bound to have an impact on me, I suppose, and it did in the end. Slowly I went to pieces.

It was absolutely awful. I started to cry myself to sleep every night. I would lie there thinking about James and Ryan and how, if they didn't have me as a mother, they would be living with their dad in a nice house.

I got to the point where I wanted to hurt myself. I just didn't want to be here any more. I began to think that if I wasn't around someone would take care of the boys. I was only holding them back. For them that couldn't have been further from the truth. They just wanted to be with their mum. But I couldn't see that.

I remember bumping into my sister-in-law in the local supermarket. She was pregnant at the time and she asked how I was getting on.

'Well,' I said. 'Apart from the fact that I wanted to kill myself last week.'

I remember the expression on her face.

Things came to a head – literally – one night.

I was sitting in my room, trying to do some studying but failing. All I could think about was how we were going to get out of this awful mess. The frustration of it all just suddenly came crashing down on me. I began bashing my head against the wall.

James came running in to see what was going on. I just looked at him and he looked at me. At that moment I thought, I'm going to have to do something about this or I will end up doing something really silly.

I made a decision to go and see a doctor. This was a big step for me because, given my pride, I'm not the kind of person who readily admits she can't cope. The GP put me on anti-depressants and the medication had an almost immediate impact, but not in the way I'd hoped: it turned me into a zombie.

I would get up in the morning and take the kids to school without even getting dressed. I would put on a coat over my pyjamas and jump into the car, drive the boys to school, then drop them off without getting out of the car. I would go back to the hostel, get back into bed and stay there all day. I did that for three weeks.

I wasn't eating much. I probably wasn't looking after the children particularly well. But friends were helping me a lot. Graham, in particular, was a godsend. He came to see me one day and took me to the shop. He said I needed a change of scenery, which was so true.

When we got there, he opened my handbag, took out my anti-depressants and threw them away. 'You're not taking them any more,' he said. 'They are not doing you any good.'

He took me into his treatment room and he did energy healing work on me. I felt lighter afterwards. My head wasn't so foggy. I caught sight of myself in the mirror and suddenly thought, 'Oh, I should have brushed my hair this morning.'

Being there for the day somehow lifted my energy. I hadn't been focusing at all since I'd started taking the medication.

There were other things adding to my unhappiness during this time; in particular, my relationship with my father had suffered over the months. He hadn't had much to do with me since we'd moved into the hostel. He thought I was wrong to wait for a council flat on what he called 'some scummy council estate'. He thought I was being stubborn, which, of course, I was.

He and Heather didn't like what I was doing with my career either. Heather had said some negative things about me working at 'Charmed'.

And money was also an issue. I didn't have any, basically.

If I had had a regular income I would have lost the benefits I was eligible for while I was homeless, which the boys and I couldn't afford to do without. To pay to live at the hostel would have cost us £600 a month, which was a ridiculous sum of money given that a council flat cost around £250 a month. So I gave away all the money I made from my readings to the shop. My view was why should I pay £600 a month to be punished by staying in the hostel? This meant, however, that we were as poor as church mice.

How we got through every day I don't know. My poor kids. Slowly but surely, living at the hostel was affecting the boys too. Ryan put on a lot of weight, as did I because we were living off rubbish. Instead of proper meals we were living off McDonalds and takeaways. There was very little in the kitchen, and there weren't any decent shops in the area to buy food.

It was just horrible living there. The boys didn't have any freedom. There wasn't anywhere to play outside. There was an alleyway that ran alongside the hostel where I didn't feel safe during the day let alone at night, so I wouldn't let them out most of the time. All the time, I kept thinking, 'I'm a bad mother; I've put my kids here, what's wrong with me?'

Our weekends with Adam became our only respite. Leaving the hostel on a Friday evening to go there felt like escaping from prison.

The lowest point came when they re-housed Jane, who had been sharing the hostel with me. Jane wanted to live in nearby Wormley and I wanted to live in Hoddesdon; however, they housed Jane in Hoddesdon before they housed me, even though she'd come into the hostel after me and I'd been given emergency points because of my depression.

I was so incensed by this I went to the local newspaper, the *Hertfordshire Mercury*, which ran a story about me. I explained that I felt we were stuck, and that whatever I tried we were trapped.

For a brief while I even considered backing down and going to live with my parents.

Sue, my cousin, had split up with her partner. She was also looking to be given a council flat for her and her two young girls. In her case, she was going through a programme called homeless at home. She was allowed to live with her parents while still accumulating points to get council accommodation.

It sounded like a good idea but I soon discovered I wasn't allowed to do that because I'd already entered the waiting list under another scheme. I was told that if I took myself out of the hostel then as far as they were concerned I wasn't their responsibility any more.

That tipped me over the edge again briefly. But after what had happened before I was determined to get myself straight without turning to medication again. I had to, for the boys' sake more than mine.

By now I had also been forced to quit University. It was just beyond me, emotionally and financially.

I knew I needed some kind of support and so I found the name of a counsellor in the Yellow Pages. I was still too paranoid to see a normal doctor. I was worried that if I started talking about how I spoke with dead people I might be locked up. They might decide I was an unfit mother and get social services involved. The idea of the boys being taken into care was too awful to even contemplate. That would have been the end of me.

So I chose a lady who did Reiki healing. She seemed slightly alternative and sympathetic to what I was doing. In fact, she was great. From the first session I had with her I felt I could talk openly about everything, including the psychic side of my life. It was very different to the talking I'd done at University, where I'd never really been able to talk freely about that important part of my life.

Within a few weeks I felt I was on the road to recovery. As well as going to the circle that I sat in with Barry and Graham, I established my own circle. It worked out well, and I soon had a regular group of around twenty people.

I also broke up with Adam. His negativity about my interest in the psychic world had grown rather than faded. He had also tried to pressure me into moving in with him. I was very fond of him. But I knew I had to stand on my own two feet.

It was while I was doing a reading for a woman who was having relationship problems that I realised it wasn't meant to be between Adam and me. The reading also told me something really important about the way this gift of mine worked.

I was using Native American cards, similar to the ones that Tony Eagletree had used on me at that fateful psychic fair. These were animal cards.

It became clear that this lady was having trouble with a man. She was quite a successful businesswoman. She was very bright and I could see she was a determined person. He didn't approve of what she was doing, however. He was being extremely negative and disapproved of seemingly everything she said and did when it came to her career.

I realised this sounded very similar to Adam's attitude towards me. He had continued to run down what I was doing. At the same time, he had become more persistent in asking me to move in with him.

When I turned over the next card I saw the image of an owl. This was a card I knew well. It was associated with the number 21. Suddenly my head was filled with thoughts not about the lady but about me. Well, me and Adam to be precise.

'He was born on 21 March,' I said.

She was stunned. 'How the hell do you know that?' she said. I didn't tell her that that was Adam's birthday as well.

I carried on talking about Adam and me. 'He says that you shouldn't listen to those people who are boosting your confidence and saying you can succeed,' I said.

'Yes. Yes, that's right, he does do that,' she said.

'He says that he can look after you, but you want to be able to look after yourself – you want to be independent.'

'Absolutely,' she nodded.

I knew I couldn't take this all the way. I had to try and look at her relationship separately as well. She wasn't me and her boyfriend wasn't Adam. There were going to be differences. As I did so, I sensed that she was going to be all right. But I didn't tell her straight out that they were going to get married and have six kids. 'I think it's going to work out OK,' I said. 'I think you're going to resolve these differences.' The woman was very pleased with the reading and left happy and ready to tackle the problems she was facing.

Afterwards, I sat there analysing what had happened. I knew it had been an important reading in terms of my own development. It was a positive and a negative moment. On the negative side, I felt it confirmed what I knew about my relationship with Adam. He wasn't right for me. He was holding me back. But on the positive side it helped me begin to understand how the spirit world was communicating through me.

Until now I'd been busily trying to interpret a barrage of information. All these seemingly random thoughts, images, sights, sounds and smells were coming into my mind and I was having to make sense of them. Until now I'd been trying to work out what they meant to the people sitting in front of me. I now realised the best way to interpret them was simply to relate them to myself and the world that I knew.

It was a question of trust. I had to trust that what I said had relevance to others. It wouldn't always, I felt sure. But it was also a question of trusting the spirit world. They wanted me to get their messages across. I had to trust them to use the most effective method for doing that. The easiest way for me to communicate was by dealing in things that I understood, in fact the thing I understood best, my own life. From then on I trusted myself to use my own knowledge and experience as the foundation stone of my mediumship.

By the spring of 2003 I was feeling desperate again. Then the council contacted me to let me know that we were now at the top of the housing waiting list and that they were able to offer us a flat. For a day or so I was over the moon. But then I went to see the place. It was dire. It was on a really rough estate, and there were only two small bedrooms, one of which was a single. The boys were growing up and needed a room each. It was no better than the hostel.

It was a really tough decision to take. They warned me that if I refused it I would move back down the waiting list again.

Things at the hostel had got worse too. When Jane moved out a family of five moved in. They were asylum seekers and had a completely different attitude to hygiene and behaviour around the hostel. I often found the kitchen in a disgusting state. What made it even worse was the way they were being treated by the council. They were given a car and had all their meals ready-cooked and delivered to them while I had to fend for myself.

But I simply couldn't accept this flat. So I said no.

The decision left me feeling low again, and my nerves began to suffer once more. I was beginning to think we had no future, and that I should send the children to Tony; I should do what my mother had done and leave them with their father. So it was ironic – to say the least – that this was the moment when I was reunited with her.

I was obviously meant to see my mother again because it was the spirit world that led me to her. The process that brought her back into my life had been set in motion just before New Year the previous year.

One December evening, everyone in my circle had begun talking about an Irishwoman whose presence they could sense. It soon became clear to me that this was my Irish grandmother, my mother's mother, who Terry Eagletree had brought through when he'd read for me at the psychic fair.

People in the circle then started talking about road names and road signs. That night, and for a few nights afterwards, I kept dreaming about these roads too. I kept seeing a blue front door with a number 12 on it. I also started seeing a sign for a village called Hatfield Peverel. I eventually asked Graham if he knew where Hatfield Peverel was.

'Yes, I do,' he said.

On New Year's Eve that year he had driven me there but I'd panicked, even though I was certain my mother was in the village.

Four months on, I finally built up the courage to go to the place again. The messages had been growing stronger over the weeks and the subject kept coming up in my circle.

Even more powerfully, my boy Ryan had been having dreams about an Irish lady. 'She's old and she's got red hair, and she keeps shouting at me to go to sleep when I'm reading at night,' he told me.

It was clear the spirit world was telling me that I had to face my past.

One Friday evening, I asked Graham whether he'd take me back to Hatfield Peverel. We headed towards the same area that we'd gone to on New Year's Eve. There was a car park outside the estate where I'd sensed my mother was living. As we pulled up, I noticed a man getting out of a van. 'If he knows my mother then we are meant to be here,' I said to Graham. 'And if he doesn't, we can go home and I'm never coming back.'

Graham got out of the car and walked over to the man. I wound down the window to listen. 'Do you know a lady called Deirdre. She's Irish and some people call her Paddy,' he asked him.

'Yes, that's my partner,' the man replied.

'Did you know she's got a daughter called Tracy and another child, a son?' Graham said.

The fellow just looked at him and shook his head. 'No, she hasn't,' he said. 'She's got a daughter called Katie.' This tied in with something my nan had said years earlier when my mother had come up in conversation. She had said that someone had told her my mother had got married again and had a daughter.

I was sure this man's wife was her.

'Do you want me to go and speak to this man's partner to see if it's her,' Graham asked me.

'OK,' I said, already knowing deep down it was.

To be honest, if I'd been the one driving you wouldn't have seen me for dust at that point. This guy didn't know about me. What right did I have to go in there and turn his world upside down? Was I about to ruin someone's life?

The man told Graham to follow him so that he could speak to his lady. I sat in the car, shaking. I couldn't see the house properly because there was a bush in the way but I saw the front door open and I saw Graham standing there.

He was there for a couple of minutes before he came back.

'It's her, it's your mum,' he said. 'I spoke to her on her own and she said she does have a daughter called Tracy and a son called Terence.'

I didn't quite know what to think. My head was alive with a million thoughts. I was confused as to why Graham was getting back into the car, however. 'What's wrong?' I said. 'Why can't I go in to see her?'

'She's having her hair done at the moment,' he replied.

'What!'

'She's having her hair done with some friends from work. They've got a hairdresser in there. She wants us to wait until she's finished, then someone will come and tell us when we can see her.'

I was dumbstruck.

'Your sister's putting the kettle on,' Graham said gently, trying to console me.

I sat there in disbelief. 'It's been twenty-three years since she last saw me and now she wants me to sit outside while she's having her hair done,' I said to Graham eventually.

As it turned out, Friday night was the night she and some of her friends from work always had a hairdresser round to do their hair. It was an open house kind of thing. It would have been a bit embarrassing and awkward for her to have the daughter that she'd been estranged from for twenty-three years suddenly walk into the middle of the parlour. Her friends didn't know about me any more than her partner did.

Eventually the man, who introduced himself as Steve, reappeared and ushered us into the house. I didn't have any photographs of her and it was so long since I'd seen her that I'd completely forgotten what she looked like. All I could remember was that she was short. I wasn't expecting to see a woman who looked a lot like me. Having said that I wouldn't have known her if she'd walked past me in the street.

There was no hug or a kiss on the cheek. She didn't even get up out of her chair. The first thing she said was: 'Hello Lil.' Lil was what my Dad called me, so that shocked me straight away. Nobody else called me that.

Her daughter Katie was there too. That was extremely strange. I had a half-sister, only a year older than my son James.

My mother asked me to sit down and offered me a cup of tea. Slowly and a bit hesitantly she began telling me about the life she'd led since Terence – or Toddy as she used to call him – and I had last seen her all those years ago.

She had remarried. Her second husband had been called John and he was Katie's dad. The marriage hadn't worked out for reasons she didn't really go into and so she had divorced him. She was now with Steve and they had lived here for several years. She was now working as a nurse in a residential care home for the elderly. She said it was hard work and long hours but she enjoyed it.

To be fair, it seemed like she had really got her life together, although it didn't take her long to sum up the last twenty-three years. She was more interested in talking about the first four years of my life, and about what had happened between her and Dad all that time ago. She seemed as obsessed by the past as she had been when I'd last seen her on those occasional Sunday visits. She tried to tell me that the marriage had started to go wrong when Dad had had an affair at a party. She also tried to say that he kept me away from her when I went to live with him. I knew this wasn't true. But if that was how she justified it to herself, then that was up to her.

As I listened to her, I couldn't help thinking: 'Who cares, that's in the past.' We sat there for about half an hour, during which time there were a lot of excuses but no emotion. A lot of the time she spoke to Graham more than me.

Every now and again she'd ask about what I'd been up to. I told her I was separated from my boys' father, but I didn't really go into any details about where I was living or my work. I didn't want to give her the satisfaction. She didn't seem that interested anyway.

The only thing that did get her excited was the prospect of meeting her grandsons. She asked us to come over for Sunday lunch and I agreed we'd come the following week.

She did see me to the door, at least, although again there was no affection. She didn't kiss me goodbye or even shake my hand. I might just as easily have been a bloke who'd been round to read the gas meter.

Driving back home, I tried to come to terms with what had happened. It wasn't easy. My head was buzzing. I understood her better now than I had done years ago. I had, of course, made some of the mistakes she'd made, having a child too young and separating from the father.

I could even understand how she'd given us to my dad. I had thought about doing a similar thing. Since we'd been in the hostel I'd thought many times of ringing up Tony and asking him to take care of Ryan and James. I'd often thought he'd do a better job of caring for them than I could.

But deep down, as a mother, I knew that even if that had happened, I would have been there to see them at every possible opportunity, which she hadn't done. And for that I couldn't forgive her. I knew our relationship wasn't going to become a close one in the future, nor did it.

Despite the feelings she'd stirred up in me, I took the boys over the following weekend to meet her. She cooked us Sunday lunch. Two moments stick in my mind about that afternoon.

At one point, while my mother was in the kitchen with Steve and Katie, and we were on our own, I asked Ryan what he thought of his new nan.

'She's all right but she's an alcoholic,' he said.

'Why do you say that?' I asked, taken aback. We hadn't seen her drink while we were in the house and I had never said anything about the way she was when I was young.

'I saw her putting sherry in the trifle,' he whispered.

I laughed.

I think she probably was close to being an alcoholic when I was a kid. Then I think the booze helped her cope. But now she couldn't have done the job she was doing as a residential care nurse if she had been drinking like she used to and getting up in the morning with a can of beer. But it was weird that Ryan should say that.

Even stranger, however, was Ryan's reaction when he saw a collection of family photos on a mantelpiece. 'I know her face,' he said, pointing at a very old, faded photograph. I didn't recognise the woman. I'd never seen the photo before. Ryan asked my mother who she was when she came back into the room.

'That's my mother, your great grandmother Kathleen,' she said. 'Why?'

'She shouts at me in my dreams sometimes,' he said.

My mother was speechless.

6 | Seeing is Believing

Towards the end of the spring in 2003 I set myself up doing Tarot readings in a shop called 'The White Witch', in Waltham Abbey.

Since that eventful night at the Latton Bush Centre three years earlier, people had been telling me that I was a medium, but I didn't really believe them. Interesting things had happened, for sure, but there had been no real consistency to them. Despite my evenings with the psychic development circles, I still didn't feel as though I'd learned much more about what it really meant to be a medium.

I had an idea that I might be psychic, but again I wasn't completely sure about the nature of my gift. I knew, on the other hand, that I was able to sense what was going on in someone's life by turning Tarot cards. I had my own approach to the Tarot, but it worked and my clients were happy with the readings I gave them.

But being a fully-fledged medium seemed like something else entirely. That meant communicating directly with the spirit world. I was very sceptical about it. In fact, at that point I absolutely didn't believe in it. Whenever anyone challenged me on this, I would reply that I would have to see the spirits in order to be able to work with them.

When I said this at circle once, everyone just laughed at me. 'You can't say that,' they said.

It was while I was working at 'The White Witch' one morning that my opinion changed. In fact, it was then that I had my first true experience as a medium.

The morning began as usual, with a sitting for a middle-aged lady.

As I worked my way through the cards, however, I started to feel different, more energised. I was aware of thoughts that weren't mine. I got the sense that they were coming from a man, but I couldn't be sure. Something told me that the spirit world was putting these thoughts into my head.

I really didn't know what to do with this information so continued to focus on the cards on the table in front of me. 'Stick to what you know,' I tried to tell myself. But when I looked up to speak to the lady, I saw that I wasn't going to be able to ignore what was happening.

The lady was still sitting in front of me but her head now looked to be about three feet wide. It took me a moment to take this in. I soon saw that what had happened was that another head had appeared behind her.

It was quite an unsettling thing to see. The image was like the negative of a photograph. There was no colour in the hair or on the skin. It was just pure black and white, with shades of grey in between.

'I'm losing the plot here,' I thought to myself. But I had to remain calm for my client, so I decided simply to describe the person that I could see behind her. As I described the man's features she just nodded. 'Do you know a man who looks like this?' I asked.

'Yes, that's my father,' she said.

At this point, I could barely see her face. All I could see was the large floating head behind her. It wasn't connected to a body. It was just a head.

I didn't tell the lady that I'd seen her father right there behind her. I finished the Tarot reading in the usual way and got ready for the next appointment. I didn't say anything about this to anyone for the rest of the day. I was, however, very intrigued. 'This is interesting,' I thought to myself.

I had more readings booked in for later in the day. Inwardly I was hoping that something else would happen. I wasn't disappointed.

The final reading I had that afternoon was with a young Turkish girl. Like so many of my clients, I could tell that she was there for a reading about her love life.

I understand now how my mind and body work when I'm doing mediumship. My energy changes and I'm literally pulsing. When I'm aware of a presence, it's as if someone is bumping into my aura, as if they are trying to let me know they are there.

It had felt like that earlier that day when the head arrived. My heart had been racing. It had been an unfamiliar feeling then, but as I began to read for this girl, I felt the same thing again. 'Here we go again,' I thought to myself.

When I looked up this time, however, there was nothing visible on her face. For a moment I was a little disappointed. But then, all of a sudden, I was aware of something on my table, alongside me. It was a man's arm – a very large, very hairy man's arm. Again it was disembodied. It ended at the upper arm and wasn't connected to anything. It was just sitting there.

No-one had told me what to do with this gift. I was having to feel my way into it on my own. So again I simply worked with what was in front of me. 'Do you know a man who has got really, really hairy arms?' I wondered. 'Even his fingers are hairy.'

The girl had just wanted a Tarot reading about her love life, as I had when I'd sat down with Tony Eagletree years earlier. So at first she was a little thrown by this change in the direction of the reading. She looked puzzled. 'That's my uncle,' she said. 'He passed two years ago. Why?'

I told her that he was trying to get in touch and that he was all right in the spirit world.

She seemed quite pleased with this information. It must have meant something to her. But at that point I really didn't know where to take this kind of reading, so I decided to play safe and returned to finishing the more mundane Tarot reading that she had come for.

As I headed home that afternoon my head was exploding. I was excited but also a little wary. 'I can see dead heads; I can see dead arms. What's going on?' one part of me was saying.

Another part of me wondered whether I was going mad, whether perhaps my brain had been affected by the medication I'd taken briefly. What else could explain this sudden arrival of these people?

But the more sensible side of me was telling me that this was serious – that I was tapping into something incredibly powerful. It was also telling me that it was something that had to be handled with care and respect.

If I really was a medium, as everyone had been telling me,

then this gift wasn't something to be messed around with. I mustn't play with it any more.

Yet another part of me, of course, was wondering whether this was a flash in the pan, a one-off moment that I'd never experience again. It wasn't long before I discovered it wasn't.

I went to my old circle the following week as normal. I felt it was important and that I might get some clues about what was going on. Almost as soon as we sat down, however, I became aware of people arriving behind the circle members. Again they were all in negatives, like the figure of the father I'd seen the previous Saturday.

Until that point, I hadn't really grasped the fact that, in relying purely on the circle for guidance, I was being taught by some mediums who weren't necessarily fully developed themselves. Until then, I'd assumed that the senior members of the group, Barry, Graham and the others, would be able to see everything that I could see. But as I watched this collection of spirits encircling us, I suddenly realised the other members of the circle weren't responding to them. They definitely weren't seeing what I could see.

I was reluctant to say anything in case they didn't know what was happening. But my body language and the way I was looking around me must have given the game away. I think it was Barry who said to me eventually, 'What are you seeing, what are you looking at?'

I knew what I wanted to say: 'I can see a man standing behind you and it feels like your dad.' That was what I was feeling. But instead I said something about the light being very strange in the room and then changed the subject.

I didn't want to acknowledge what was going on, because I was in a room full of mediums and I was the baby there. They were the professionals and I was an amateur. I spent the rest of the evening watching the spirits gathered all around us, not letting on that I could see them.

Again a million thoughts were going through my head, but this time they were all focused in one direction. This really was happening. I wasn't going mad. After all the doubts I had had, it seemed that I was indeed somehow blessed with an ability as a medium. I now had to begin to learn more about putting that ability to use.

In June 2003, a member of my circle, Ellie, organised a trip to see a show in London. The show was 'The Three Mediums', featuring Colin Fry, Derek Acorah and Tony Stockwell, and it was being staged at the Hammersmith Apollo.

It seemed to me the perfect opportunity to see the very best mediums at work, and it was also a fun night out with friends. There were ten of us in all, so a couple of the better-off girls decided to hire a limo. I was all for going on the train and bus, but I think they knew I needed cheering up and so they also bought some champagne on the journey. We were all in a very good mood by the time we got to Hammersmith.

All of us were really looking forward to the show. Since acknowledging that I had mediumistic abilities, I'd begun to study the work of some of the most prominent mediums, in particular Colin Fry, star of the new television series *6ixth Sense* and the American medium John Edward, whose videos

Graham had first lent to me and who I really loved watching
in action. I had also seen Derek Acorah on the show *Most
Haunted*. One or two of the girls had heard of Tony
Stockwell, although I hadn't at that point.

There were about 3,500 people crammed into the
Hammersmith Apollo. There were a lot of celebrities there,
including Melinda Messenger, Daniella Westbrook and a
few reality television stars. The show was being filmed for
television.

It was a massive auditorium yet there was a very quiet,
reverential atmosphere. At a normal theatre or music show
people take their seats and chat away and eat crisps or
whatever. It wasn't like that at all here. Everyone was talking
in whispers, sitting quietly. We were all very much focused
on what was going on.

When the three mediums appeared I remember being in
awe of all of them. I was blown away by the fact that they
were going to practise their mediumship in front of so many
people.

As the show got under way, I tried to take in everything
that was happening. For me it wasn't just about enjoying the
messages; it was looking at the whole process – it was about
how these men could stand on stage and do what they did. I
was mesmerised by the fact that they were able to doing this
live on stage. There wasn't any part of me that doubted what
I was witnessing. The whole experience left me transfixed.

I decided to watch out for who would get messages by
looking for lights above these people's heads. I don't think I
moved throughout the whole two hours.

What really interested me was the fact that each of the
mediums had different ways of working. Colin seemed more

quiet and in control. He worked with great precision and you had to keep an eye on him and listen in case you missed something. I'd seen him on television and been impressed, but seeing this live took the experience to a different level. I could see why he had the reputation he did as a stage medium.

Tony was slightly different. He worked by building the evidence he was getting from the spirit world and then placing it with someone in the audience. He was a bit quicker and machine gun-like than Colin, which was something I could identify with. That was the way I'd experienced things. They had come very fast into my head. If I was ever going to do stage mediumship I felt I would have to get my information out fast – before it went.

Derek, on the other hand, was very dramatic. Of the three, he was the most flamboyant character, and that came across in his readings. I remember that Derek gave a message at one point by shouting out, 'Mr Wilson, I've got Mr Wilson.' It turned out to be a teacher who was trying to get in touch with an ex-pupil in the audience.

The pupil was a man. He probably wasn't a sceptic but was definitely what we call a 'dragalong' – someone who has been brought along against his will by a partner. His reaction was amazing. He was blown away.

At the end of the show all three mediums got a standing ovation. It was a hell of a show. Afterwards we all queued up to meet them, where they were signing books and autographs in the foyer.

When we reached the head of the queue I found myself talking to Tony Stockwell. I liked some of the pendulums they were selling and asked him where they got them from.

It turned out that the supplier was somebody I knew. As we chatted further I found out that Tony was quite local to me in Wickford in Essex. I also discovered that he taught classes, and I took some literature about them away.

Heading back home that night I began imagining myself doing mediumship. Could I do it? Did I have the courage and the ability to stand up in front of an audience like that? Where could I find the guidance I needed?

What I was picturing was on a smaller scale, of course.

If someone had said to me that in April 2009 you too will be on that stage, in front of 3,500 people at the Hammersmith Apollo, as one of the three mediums I would have told them they were a complete lunatic.

Finally, in September 2003, the boys and I were re-housed. We had been in the hostel for eighteen months, but it had felt like a life sentence. We were all elated to be out of there.

We were offered a flat on an estate in the nearby town of Wormley. We were so excited to get out of the hostel that when we got our first glimpse of our new home it seemed absolutely ideal. It was a flat with three bedrooms on quite a large, well laid-out estate, with a lot of open spaces. There was plenty of green space at the front of the house where the boys could play. During the daytime it was a lovely place to be. The problem was that during the night it was hell.

The estate was full of real tearaways. Even the pizza delivery boys were getting mugged, so now they refused to deliver to the flats after a certain time in the evening. And it didn't take long for the local bad boys to target the newcomers.

It was partly because my boys refused to join them. When I think about it, I was so lucky. My kids could have ended up on drugs. They could have joined gangs or turned to drink. But they never did. Rather than feeling low or depressed about living in the conditions we had been in, they had learned to deal with it in their own ways.

James was musical and, at the age of fourteen, had started to write songs about his experiences. Ryan would just spend all his time drawing. He was pretty easy going. As long as he had a bed and his belly was full nothing seemed to affect him much.

Neither of them was interested in joining the gang on the estate. So they were soon being spat at and jeered at by the local bullies.

I suffered just as much. The moment I drove on to the estate, if I was spotted by one of the gang that was it. The next morning the windscreen of my car would be smashed or the wing mirrors ripped off. The kids were little buggers.

However, I wasn't going to let these people ruin our new lives. I was determined that we were going to make up for the year and a half we'd effectively lost while we were stuck in the hostel.

Soon after we arrived in Wormley it was James's birthday. He was fifteen. We'd not been able to have a party while we were at the hostel so we splashed out and threw one, inviting a few neighbours. I felt like a real mum again, making sure there was plenty of pizza and drinks, baking a cake and generally fussing over the arrangements. But in the event all the kids who lived on the estate invited themselves to the party – even the ones we didn't know. At one point, one little hooligan threatened to cut off my face.

I just couldn't believe it. We had jumped out of the frying pan into the fire. At one point James and I agreed we'd rather be back in the hostel than in our new home. It was very depressing.

Fortunately the boys could spend time with their father every now and again. It did them good to get away from London – and from Wormley. Their weekends with Tony also gave me a chance to try to develop my mediumship.

In November, Ellie, who had organised the trip to see 'The Three Mediums', was given a lovely present by her husband. It was a weekend's course with Tony Stockwell in Canterbury. She asked me if I fancied going along with her. It was just what I needed, so I booked myself a place on the course as well.

I was immediately impressed by Tony Stockwell. I'd been in awe of him and the other mediums at the Hammersmith Apollo. But away from that showbiz environment he was a very down-to-earth guy. He wasn't one of those mystical, airy-fairy characters who you sometimes came across in the psychic world. He was spiritual and had a great energy, and was also a patient teacher. But he had no airs and graces. I liked that.

During one of the sessions that weekend he made me stand up in the classroom and try mediumship. I was very nervous. I'd never tried to connect with the spirit world in a group like this before. But I immediately felt a strong presence.

Tony saw this. 'So what have you got?' he said.

'A man. I'm getting a strong feeling about the name

Russell. He's a dad, not a real dad, a step-dad or a foster dad. Something like that. He died of a heart attack and that's all I know,' I said.

To be honest, I'd not liked the sensations I was getting. I didn't like the feeling of grief this man had been giving me. So I sat down. I'd been concentrating so hard I'd not been looking at Tony or the rest of the class. When I looked at my friends they were staring at Tony. And he was staring at me.

'What is it?' I wanted to know. Inside I was thinking: 'You're one of The Three Mediums. Surely you were able to see what I just did too?'

'Have you done that before?' he asked after a moment.

'No.'

'You sure?'

'Yes. Positive. I'm here to learn mediumship. I'm a beginner really.'

'Well, that's a very impressive first attempt then,' he said. He explained, 'My adopted father was called Russell. He died a few years ago of a heart attack.'

There was a mild ripple of applause from my friends, but elsewhere in the class I could sense some negativity. They probably thought I'd read up on Tony or something, which I hadn't of course.

Afterwards I spoke to Tony a bit more about what had happened. He was very supportive and he repeated the same sort of things that Barry had said three years earlier. He told me I was going to be a demonstrating medium. I was going to be famous for it. I was amazed again, but this time even more so. After all, this was now coming from a famous medium.

Since I'd had my first experience with the disembodied

head and the hairy arm during my Tarot readings, I had often felt or seen something during my readings. If I was sure of what it was or what it meant I would tell the person I was reading for.

These experiences had started to mount up. And the more I trusted what I was feeling, it seemed the more I got back. It was like a reward. I had begun to feel that if you give the spirit world something it gives you more in return.

That weekend was a real turning point for me. It gave me the confidence to be among other people who practised mediumship. I felt I was as good as any of them.

7 | Taking Flight

One morning I was sitting on the bed in the flat when the phone went. 'Is that Tracy Higgs?' a voice asked.

'Yes.'

'You contacted us about getting some work with our agency. We were wondering if you could come in for an interview.'

A friend of mine had suggested that I get in touch with an agency which was well known for representing mediums, astrologers and psychics, and which found them work in the media, magazines and sometimes television. My friend was on their books and had found them very professional. She had also got a fair bit of work from them.

I saw no harm in giving it a try, so I had sent them some details. Since my experience with Tony Stockwell in Canterbury a month earlier, I was growing in confidence and was ready to spread my wings a bit. I immediately said yes to the interview and agreed to visit them at their offices in Maidstone, Kent.

As a new face, I didn't expect to get much work to begin with. I knew they supplied psychics for corporate events when companies wanted to book people to give readings at Christmas parties and stuff like that. And I also knew they had some links to the media, but I didn't think that was something they'd use me for. I had no expectations. I was just pleased to be asked along for an interview. It was a much needed boost to my confidence.

I had other reasons for approaching them too. Living in Wormley continued to be a nightmare. There was one particular family for whom we were a specific target. If a window cleaner came round to wash the windows, the minute he'd gone they would pelt them with eggs. On one side of the house on the ground floor we didn't dare open the curtains, even during the day. If we did, they would set fire to the bin room near us.

The attacks happened all the time. On one occasion, I had just finished decorating the flat with new wallpaper, to make it look nice and homely for the kids. But because the firemen had had to wet the walls to put out the most recent fire, water came through the walls.

In contacting the agency, I also wanted to prove a point to my ex-boyfriend Adam. We'd been in touch again and he'd again run down what I was doing. He would say things like: 'You should give up on this. You'll never be on television, you'll never get anywhere with it. You're not confident enough and you shouldn't listen to those people who say you can do this.'

I was determined to prove him wrong.

Nevertheless, I travelled down to the agency's studios for my interview with low expectations. I decided there was no point in dressing up, so I just turned up in a casual shirt and jeans. I decided to go just as I was and to be myself. I was very fatalistic about it. If it was meant to be, it was meant to be.

When I arrived, I met three different people – Robin, Suzie and Alan. They asked me various questions about my work and videoed me during the interview. When the interview was over I asked them why they'd needed to put it on film. I was never afraid to ask questions.

'We needed to do that to see what you're like on film. Some people are more photogenic and better on camera than others,' Robin explained.

'That was a waste of time, then,' I laughed.

Robin looked at me, slightly confused. 'Don't you know?' he said.

'Don't I know what?'

'The camera loves your face.'

'What?'

He smiled patiently. 'You will look good on screen and film.'

I thought he was just sucking up to me. I guessed that I was a good enough psychic for them to put me on their books, but I thought he was flattering me.

To my amazement, Robin told me that they'd like to sign me up there and then. There was no going away and thinking about it.

They offered me a deal where they took a percentage of the fees for any work they generated for me. They couldn't guarantee work, obviously.

'If anything comes up we will let you know,' they said, as I shook their hands and said goodbye.

A lot of people think you sign up with an agent and that's it. The work pours in. I didn't. I just thought that, 'If it comes up it comes up.' But it really was that simple. From that day onwards I didn't stop working. I was busy all the time.

My first assignment was for the magazine *Spirit and Destiny* for a column called 'Psychic House Detectives'.

I was asked to go to a house in Notting Hill with a medium called Judy Jones. The house was empty and we had to see what we could deduce about who lived there. She looked at it her way while I looked at it my way. We both went into the different rooms, the bedrooms. It was a bit like a psychic version of *Through The Keyhole*: 'Who lives in a house like this?'

My job was to read the place psychically. I did pretty well. I got the woman's name, what she did for a living, and quite a few details about what she was like.

The flat was gorgeous, odd but beautiful. I kept seeing people with cameras knocking on her door all the time. It turned out that the flat was used a lot by film crews and for photo shoots, and the woman who lived there was an actress.

I really enjoyed the experience. I found it easy and fun to do and the magazine people were easy to work with. It began a relationship with them that would last for years.

What was really nice about working with them was that you never felt as if you had to prove something. If you went somewhere and didn't get anything they would take your professional word for it. They wouldn't tell you just to make something up.

I wrote a column called 'Psychic SOS' for them for a long time, along with Michèle Knight and Robin from the agency.

By far the most exciting assignment the agency got for me was on *The X Factor* spin-off show, *The Xtra Factor*.

I was invited on the show in October to analyse some doodles that various contestants had done. They asked me to look at the drawings and pick out the four that I thought stood out. It was filmed 'as live'.

The producers were a bit annoyed with me because I hadn't been watching the show and didn't know the exact line up of acts remaining in the contest. I did usually watch, but life in Wormley had been so grim lately that I'd spent a lot of weekends away from there and my television.

But I went ahead anyway and did what they wanted, choosing a quartet of drawings. But I also singled out one in particular. 'The winner drew this,' I said.

This took the film crew a bit by surprise. 'How do you know that?' the presenters asked.

'It's obvious, if you look at it,' I said.

The artist had drawn a snowman, a big house and a celebration in the corner. To me it was clear what it represented. The show finished at Christmas. Here was someone who wanted a solid home, and desperately wanted to win this competition.

'It's all coming out in the drawing,' I said.

It turned out that the drawing had been done by Shayne Ward, one of the favourites to win the competition. And it made even more sense to me when I finally caught up with the show again. I found out that Shayne came from a broken home and may even have had a relative in prison. No wonder he was yearning for the solidity of a nice home.

That Christmas I managed to watch the final. And Shayne won, as I predicted.

The 'Xtra Factor' experience went down well with *The Xtra Factor* and, in particular, with the agency. They promised me there would be lots more television work as a result of that appearance.

The good news was that the work I was getting from the agency allowed me to continue with my development. I was always thinking: 'I need to know more. I need to be pushed more. I'm not good enough yet.'

Tony Stockwell ran monthly sessions in Wickford, Essex where he had a studio. I signed up for as many of them as I could afford, and I found that I had a knack for most of the disciplines he taught.

With Tony, I did more work on understanding my spirit guide. I learned that Paddy – the man with the beard who had appeared on that first night in Barry's circle – was a nineteenth-century Irish potato farmer.

Most importantly, as I began to develop, discover and explore my gift, I slowly began to understand it properly. It became clear that I'm a clairvoyant medium. This means that I can see and receive messages from the spirit world. That is what clairvoyance means: clear seeing. It explained how I had been able to see colours and the darkening around the eyes when I was a young girl.

I'm also clairsentient, which means I can feel everything that the spirit I'm connecting with has felt. So, for instance, I can feel the illness or condition that led to that person's passing. I can also feel their emotions. This was what I'd experienced during that very first circle with Barry when I'd felt the blood draining from someone's arm.

As well as being clairsentient, I'm clairaudient, which means I can hear the spirit world, although not always objectively. Sometimes what I hear is in my mind.

And I'm clairknowing, which means I sometimes have thoughts in my mind that aren't mine. These are direct thoughts from the spirit world. This was an ability that had always been there, even in my childhood. I'd simply not understood what it was – until now.

Finally, I'm clairaugustan, which means I can smell and taste the spirit world. For instance, in the presence of a spirit I can experience strong smells, anything from the pungent aroma of a wet dog to the bitter taste of a cigarette.

The more I learned, the more excited I became. It was exhilarating.

The next big breakthrough came, however, when I attended another week-long course with which Tony Stockwell was involved, this time at the famous Arthur Findlay College.

Set in a beautiful old building in lovely gardens in the middle of the Essex countryside near Stansted, the Arthur Findlay College is the country's leading psychic and mediumship training centre. People travel from all over the world to study and spend time there. It's a real haven, a place I fell in love with immediately.

I had booked myself onto the week-long course, expecting to be included in the same sort of beginners' class as at Tony Stockwell's studio. But when I looked up my class details on the Monday morning, I saw that I had been put into an advanced group with established platform mediums.

As soon as I saw this I panicked and went to find Tony. 'I've been put in the wrong class,' I complained. 'It's full of platform mediums. I'm nowhere near ready for that; I'm just here to learn how to be a medium.'

Tony just laughed at me. 'Just go with it,' he said. 'You'll be fine.'

He explained that the spirit world had already decided which classes we were going to be in – and that we were not to argue about it.

The class was being run by a Scottish lady called Eileen Davies. I liked her immediately; she had a lovely, gentle energy about her. When Eileen went around the class asking us all what we'd done I told her that I worked as a one-to-one reader, mainly doing psychic readings and I wanted to develop my mediumship.

On hearing this, she gave me a slightly funny look as if to say 'I wasn't expecting you in my class.'

However, on the first day, we did an exercise during which we all had to stand on a platform blindfolded. I was one of the first to go.

Eileen stood me on the platform and blindfolded me. She reminded the rest of the class that no-one else was allowed to talk apart from her and me. If the recipient of a message accepted any information they would simply nod and Eileen would say, 'Yes,' on their behalf.

There were no other voices in the room. I was completely blind in every sense. And I was really nervous, and shaking like mad. The energy was very strong, however, and I was soon able to focus.

Before long I sensed a presence: that of a father whose daughter was now twenty-four years old. I could feel him talking on stage to people; I could also feel a powerful pain in my side. He was very sick before he died. As I was coming out with this stream of information, all I could hear from Eileen was: 'Yes, yes, yes.'

Once again, as when I'd done my first palm and Tarot readings, I honestly felt as though I was just making up a story. I was simply working through what I was feeling. But, as I'd learned, it was fine to trust my gut instincts. They'd served me well enough so far.

I felt there was a man there, standing very close to me. I could feel it in my body and I was thinking it in my mind. People often ask me how I know this. The best comparison I can make is when someone is standing behind you and you sense they are there. And you normally have a sense whether it's a man or a woman because you can sense their energy. That's how it feels to me.

I passed on some more information that he gave me. He was an alcoholic and had died of liver failure. He hadn't been gone very long.

When Eileen took off the blindfold I was amazed to see that I had turned my body so that I was focusing my energy directly towards a girl in the class. She was quite young and quirky, not at all like the older more staid types who were also on the course. She looked drained, as if she'd been crying.

'How many times have you done that?' Eileen asked me.

'I've never done it before,' I replied.

She gave me a searching look.

'Honestly,' I confirmed.

It turned out that the reading had been very accurate. The experience of standing on a platform that I'd described referred to when the man had stood on a platform at his AA meetings. He had also said something about being proud of her when she stood on platforms, which she was now doing as a practising medium.

At the end the class all clapped. I felt slightly over-whelmed. There were people in this class who had been doing platform or stage mediumship for ten years. These people had been performing for audiences all over the country. It was then that it really dawned on me that this could be a career.

Eileen was fantastically supportive. Afterwards she said the same thing to me that Barry and Tony Stockwell and others had said. This time, however, I finally began to believe it. She said, 'You're going to be a teacher; you're going to be an ambassador for the spirit world.'

I didn't know what to say to that.

During that week I began to watch the way other mediums worked. I was able to spend time observing the way they were on stage, how they interacted with people in their audience and how they put their evidence together. As I did so, I often thought, 'Yes, I like that, no I don't like that.'

I saw lots of different styles. Some were like Doris Stokes, and spoke directly to spirit, a style that to me now seemed very out of date. Others went out there and seemed very lazy in what they did. I watched them and thought, 'Where are the names, where is the direct evidence?'

And others were extremely slow. It was almost like pulling teeth, when they gave evidence. To my mind this wasn't modern mediumship, at least not the kind I was interested in practising. In fact, I even had doubts about whether it was mediumship at all. In my experience the spirit world resonated very quickly. If your messages weren't forming fast then you were not in touch with spirit, as far as I was concerned.

In a way I began to see that mediumship was a bit like the internet. Some mediums were still operating dial-up, while the world was waiting for broadband.

Of all the mediums I watched that week, the one whose style I admired most was Eileen Davies. Her evidence was so strong and she dealt in absolute specifics, which was something I believed was vitally important.

I'd met a couple of platform mediums in the past who had appalled me with their attitude to accuracy. 'Oh, if you keep it general there's always someone out there to take your evidence,' one of them had said to me. 'For instance, if you offer the name George, there's always an Uncle George to get you started.'

I made a decision there and then that I wouldn't perform in such a cynical way. That week I promised myself that I wouldn't put myself in front of large audiences until I could do it as well as Eileen, with as much detail and specifics as she brought through.

My only problem was getting experience. And experience was everything.

The spiritualist churches were the traditional places in which to cut your teeth as a medium. But that door wasn't open to me. The spiritualist churches had very strict rules. People were required to have sat in a circle for at least three years before offering readings; they had to be recommended by members of a church, that sort of thing. This simply wasn't an option as far as I was concerned.

To be honest, it didn't bother me. I had – and still have – the utmost respect for the spiritualist movement. Some of the most generous, kind and warm people I've met during my work have been members of the movement. But, like any large movement, there are bound to be bad apples and I'd met one of them when I'd been working at 'Charmed' a few years earlier.

I'd read that there was going to be an open day, featuring quite a well known spiritualist medium. I won't mention his name here but he was regarded as a top medium in the UK at the time. I haven't heard much about him in recent years, for reasons that I now understand.

In the week or so leading up to the open day I was so excited. I couldn't wait to see him in action. I was still living with the boys in the hostel at the time, and so I was hoping someone like my Pops would make contact and give me some guidance on what to do, how to get myself out of there.

It was soon clear that I'd chosen the wrong person to ask. When I sat down with this man he began by describing all these guides he could see. There were Native Americans,

Egyptians, monks and even a nun in there. Who wasn't there wasn't worth talking about.

This wasn't what I wanted.

So while he was going through all this, I looked up and saw my great grandad, my Pops, sitting there at the side of the room, watching me. It was as if he was saying, 'Don't pay too much attention to this chap, he doesn't know anything'.

As the reading went on the chap started talking about cats. I was more of a dog person myself. 'The only cats I knew were the dead ones which had tried to get too near my dad's pigeons and had been shot,' I told him.

He didn't really appreciate my sense of humour. He also didn't accept that he was off the mark. 'Oh no, this cat loves you,' he insisted. He had seen me in the shop the day before the reading so perhaps he had figured that I was a spiritual woman and therefore I must have a cat.

Wrong.

All I wanted to know from him was when I was going to leave the hostel. So I came right out and explained my situation to him. 'When am I going to get out of there?' I asked. And I couldn't resist telling him that I'd seen a spirit in the room. 'I know there is spirit here, so please can you just ask them when I can expect to get a council flat?'

He really didn't like this and snapped: 'You don't deserve to get out of there. Women like you; all you do is taunt men. So where you're at the moment is where you're meant to be – and where you will stay.'

I stormed out. He was insinuating that I was some kind of slut or something.

I went straight round to see Graham. 'I can't believe he's just said that,' I gasped, still in a state of shock at what I'd heard. 'And that's a person who is supposed to be a leading spiritualist medium.'

At that point I'd made a vow. 'I'll never set foot in that church again as long as that man runs it. No way. Over my dead body,' I said.

And I never did.

As I immersed myself in the world of mediumship that week, I recounted this episode to the other mediums at the Arthur Findlay College. They shook their head in disbelief.

The more I talked to my colleagues there, however, the clearer it became that they didn't think I was right for the traditional world of mediumship anyway.

'Well, you're not a twin-set and pearls kind of girl,' Tony Stockwell smiled when I asked him about it. What he meant was that I didn't conform to the old school of mediumship.

As I developed, I began to see that this could work in my favour. It could make me different. I could be a thoroughly modern medium.

I should make it clear here that I have absolutely nothing against the Spiritualist Church or indeed any other Churches. It's the idea that a church is the only place in which you can find the spirit world that I have a problem with.

I was quite religious as a girl. I attended Sunday school and was even a member of the Christian Union at school. And I still love going to churches. But I don't think you have to go to church for God to be close to you. Why do you have to go to a particular building to find him? Why can't he be in the pub over the road?

When James was born he was christened at a C. of E. church in Yorkshire because of his grandmother. Ryan wasn't christened, however, and I remember the padre in the Army telling me once that he was a devil child. 'You need to pray because the devil is going to come and get him,' he said to me once.

I was quite blunt with him. 'I can pray to God in the toilet just as easily as I can pray in your church. God isn't going to care where I'm doing my praying.'

I think the same thing applies to mediumship. When you go to a spiritualist church you're literally preaching to the converted. All the lovely people in there are very spiritual, they know what you're doing and get what you're doing. But I believe that you can feel the spirit world anywhere. And what's more if you go out into theatres or hire a local hall, whatever it may be, you can have people in there who have never seen a medium before and who have no idea what mediumship is all about.

As my week at the College drew to a close I made my mind up that I would rather reach out to those people. I knew that I needed to be a medium who took the messages from the spirits out into the wider world.

It was now a matter of getting out there.

I left the College on a high. I really felt like I was flying. The week I'd spent there had almost been a 'Road to Damascus' experience for me.

I was soon brought crashing down to earth, however. Life had become increasingly unhappy living in Wormley. The neighbours' persecution of us had become even worse. One day we arrived home to discover that the porch was covered in mud. They had smeared it all the way up the curtains and the door. It was everywhere. We reported it to the police but they didn't do anything. Ryan in particular was too scared to go outside on his own. I'd got him a dog, a Rottweiler, but the gangs had tried to steal it.

The council refused to help me. It didn't matter what I said. They didn't seem to care. I realised that I had to work my backside off again so that we could get out. We had to move again.

When Ryan turned thirteen in April 2005 he went off to spend a weekend with his dad. While he was away James and I decided to make him a room of his own. There was a huge walk-in cupboard, which we didn't really use. We cleared it out, painted it and decorated it with posters. It was to be Ryan's own space. We even bought him a new bed as well.

So when he came back James and I showed him into his room and said: 'Surprise'.

Except it was Ryan who gave us the real surprise. He just looked at me sadly and told me he couldn't live with us any more. He wanted to go and live with his father back up in Yorkshire.

It took me a couple of days to get over the shock. I was heartbroken. My friends told me that I had to insist he stayed. I had to tell him I was his mother and his place was with me. But I couldn't do that to him. I wanted my children to have their own voice and to be independent. I didn't want anyone telling him what to do. So I talked it over with Tony and I agreed that he could go.

James was going to be eighteen that year but Ryan was my

baby. And he was moving out. I cried for two days when he left.

In the winter of 2004 I had got a call about a new television channel that was launching. My agents wanted to know whether I would be interested in being one of the regular psychics on the channel. It would involve me appearing live on air, reading cards, doing readings from text messages that were sent in, that sort of thing. It sounded all right so I said I would give it a go.

The show started in February 2005. The lady who owned the station was a friend of a friend and I had met her once or twice. The other presenter was the daughter of a newspaper reporter I knew; I had read for her family in the days when I was based at 'Charmed' in Cheshunt. We worked together well on screen.

At first it was really good fun. The format wasn't exactly complicated. It consisted of the two of us in a room, talking about the things that interested us, the Tarot and other readings. I didn't even think about the fact there was a camera on. I really enjoyed it. I felt relaxed and at home on the set.

It was hard work, though. At one point I had my own show on Wednesdays. It ran from 9 in the morning until 9 at night, with just twenty minutes for lunch. Being on television for twelve hours non-stop was exhausting. And the show had to be live because we were there to answer people's questions.

Although I really enjoyed it at first, there were soon signs that things were changing, and not necessarily for the better.

We did a Valentine's Night special where we were sent lots of questions from single people who were hoping to find out when they were going to meet someone. This was the sort of thing I was comfortable doing. I'd got a bit of a reputation as a reader who helped couples with relationship problems.

The show went well for the first few hours, but after a while I suddenly realised that some of the questions being put to me were being texted in by the producers. The questions were sexual in nature.

The way the show worked was that I was free to call for a break on air when I felt like it. When I saw these messages I asked for time out. With the cameras off, I told them exactly what I felt. 'I'm not using my gift for this. I'm here to help people – not to titillate you. I'm definitely not answering questions like that,' I said. I was really angry.

They didn't put me in that situation again, but it was soon clear that this had been the beginning of a change in direction.

Not long after the Valentine's special they started advertising a new medium. I found out when they sent out a mass text to all their subscribers, which I received as well. They were promoting him as a 'crossing over' medium. This was a phrase associated with John Edward and I didn't think it was right to use it, particularly given the person who they were promoting. I had encountered him and had taken an instant dislike to him. He didn't have a spiritual bone in his body.

I phoned the owner of the station immediately. 'I'm not happy about this,' I explained.

'Well, what are you going to do about it?' she challenged.

'I'm resigning,' I said.

She was very upset.

To be honest, I knew it was the right decision immediately. The job was taking its toll physically. I was leaving home at 7 a.m. to get to the studios in west London where it was all shot. On Wednesdays in particular I was arriving home dead to the world.

It was also mentally very tiring. Initially there had been interaction, which was an aspect I enjoyed, but that was no longer there. I knew I was making an impact because I got a lot of fan mail, but the calls weren't coming through as they once had.

I began to feel like a robot sitting there. And I didn't like that. I need to feel feedback.

The owner of the station called me one more time before I left. She was still furious. I'll never forget her final words to me. They were a bit of a showbusiness cliché. 'You will never work in television again,' she said before down slamming the receiver.

That was on the Tuesday and on the Wednesday I got a phone call to go on the *Richard and Judy Show*. It was a great experience. I was asked to do some predictions about Prince Charles and Camilla, who were just about to get married. I frightened the host, Richard Madeley, a little when, before the cameras started rolling, I admitted I didn't know what I was going to say. 'I'll read the crystals live,' I told him. 'But I don't know what they'll say until I look.'

Fortunately I didn't see anything too controversial. In fact, the reading suggested Charles and Camilla were a perfect match – something that, I think, history has since confirmed.

As I drove home that afternoon I no longer felt the same

way about my future and the station I'd just left. When I'd told them I was leaving the TV show, some of my friends had said that it would ruin my career. But in my heart I knew it wasn't what I wanted to be doing.

I knew there were better opportunities out there. And, on the very first day after walking out, I'd appeared on a show that was watched by more people in one hour than would probably view my old station if it carried on broadcasting for ten years (which I very much doubted it would).

I also knew I hadn't been true to myself during my time at the station. That definitely wasn't my destiny. I was sure my destiny lay somewhere else.

8 | A Thoroughly Modern Medium

I knew I needed to keep on developing my gift, so I started to sign up for every seminar, every course and workshop that I felt would help me. It seemed each new experience was opening up possibilities for me.

One of the most interesting and productive courses I went on was held at the College of Psychic Studies in London and was run by a leading medium called Michael Hunter. During one of the classes he asked us to try what is known as psychometry.

He gave me and the other students an envelope, which, he told us, each contained a photograph, and he wanted us to tell him what it showed.

At first I thought it was crazy. 'You're mad. How am I supposed to do that?' I laughed.

'Feel it and then psychically feel it,' he said. 'You mustn't use spirits to help you. You have to feel it and interpret it yourself.'

There were four or five other people in the class. As Michael went around them they were all coming up with these great stories about how they could imagine walking down lanes lined with trees and blue skies above.

I didn't have anything like that. When it came to my turn

I just said: 'I feel this might be an image of a man or a woman in here. I do feel a very sensitive energy. But I'm not feeling a lot psychically.'

'OK,' Michael said. 'Try going mediumistically.'

I had to put the envelope down to do this because – under the Witches Act of 1851 or some other kind of rubbish – you're not allowed to read photographs with your hands on them.

'It's definitely a man,' I said.

'How do you know that?'

'Because I can feel him standing next to me.' In my mind I could see a very respectable looking man in a blue blazer jacket with a tie. He was slightly balding. I continued, 'He liked teaching people but he never really achieved everything he wanted to in life. He had three strokes and a heart attack before he passed.'

While I was speaking, I was coming out with the first things that were in my head. I could sense a couple of the other women in the class looking at me, and I could feel that they weren't exactly feeling positive towards me. 'I hope I'm right otherwise I'm going to look a complete idiot,' I thought to myself.

The information this man was giving me was now coming through in waves. 'He is showing me my nan, whose surname is Higgs. But I feel his name must be longer. I'm also seeing an army name tag,' I said, not really knowing what any of this meant. All the same, I was quite confident that I was on the right track, so I also passed on a feeling I was getting about this man's opinion of Michael.

'I don't know if you know him,' I said to Michael, 'but he is very impressed by you.'

Michael didn't react to this but signalled to me that he'd heard enough. 'OK, open the envelope,' he added.

I pulled out a photograph of a man. 'That's him,' I said. 'That's the man I was describing. Who is he?'

Michael looked genuinely surprised. 'What do you mean, who is he? That's Gordon Higginson. How can you not know who he is?'

'Sorry, I don't know.' I looked at the photo again. 'Please tell me. Who is Gordon Higginson?'

I'm sure the other members of the class were shaking their heads at this point but I genuinely didn't know. Michael told me that Gordon Higginson was the President of the Spiritualist National Union. He was widely regarded as perhaps the most important medium this country has ever produced.

'He did serve in World War I and he did have a nametag that just had the name Higgs on it, because Higginson was too long,' he said. 'You might also like to know that while in the trenches he rather famously led a group of men to safety by following one of his spirit guides, a little negro child. And, yes, he did have three strokes and a heart attack before he died. Brilliant.'

Mike was great, and later on he gave me a load of books and tapes on Gordon Higginson.

I could tell that not every one in the class was impressed, however. It wasn't a class in which we were all rooting for each other. It was a class of individuals. There were a few people there who thought they were better than everyone else. To them, I was the odd one out.

I could feel them thinking, 'She's just showing off.' But I really wasn't showing off. I was just doing what Mike had told me to do. It was to prove a very useful lesson indeed.

As I'd discovered when I'd started out reading Tarot cards at 'Charmed', there were rules to mediumship that had to be learned. One of the first of those was that there weren't any rules.

In the traditional spiritualist medium movement people talk of strict guidelines on what can and can't happen when someone passes over. They describe, for instance, a period of adjustment when those who have passed over aren't available to communicate with mediums. Typically, according to a lot of these mediums, this can be around six months.

During one of the first mediumistic readings I did, the spirit of a lady's grandmother came through.

'Your nan's here,' I said, drawing a rather surprised look from the lady. 'She has passed over.'

'Well. Yes, she has,' she said, a bit hesitantly.

I suddenly had this overwhelming feeling of cold, as if someone had opened the door and an Arctic blast of wind had blown in. I shivered. 'It feels like she's in a fridge.'

'Yes, well, she is. She's still in the morgue. We haven't buried her yet, as she only died yesterday,' she explained.

At a demonstration in Bury St Edmunds one evening a few months later I made contact with someone who had passed over even sooner. A lady who was connecting with me kept showing me the phrase 'midday'. A relative was in the audience and recognised who I was describing.

'She died at midday,' she confirmed. 'Midday today!'

That remains the quickest I've ever known someone come through.

As my development progressed, I continued studying at the Arthur Findlay College. I found it a great place, spiritually. I could find peace there if I wanted, yet I could also tap into its huge energy too.

As I did so, I discovered even more aspects to my gift.

I believe very strongly that mediumship needs to move with the times, that it needs to reflect the way people live today. We live in the age of the internet and the iPod and mediums need to understand and tune in to that age. Curiously, I began to realise that I could use the radio and television to receive messages.

I'd suspected I'd had this ability for a few years. When I'd been living in Hoddesdon, years earlier, there had been a drive-by shooting. It happened in the morning before school. I'd dropped my boys off at school and was driving back home when I heard on the radio the name of the man who had been shot dead.

As far as I'm concerned the radio announcer said: 'A man called Dave King was shot dead at a gym in Hoddesdon this morning.' And I heard him say that the other man involved in the incident had a name like Kerry or Kelly. I remember thinking it was a girl's name.

At the time I was working at 'Charmed', and was in the early stages of my development. It was all still new to me and I had my doubts about whether it was something I should even be pursuing.

When I got home I rang my cousin Sue. She had had

children with a man called Brendan King, so I asked her whether the dead man was a relative of his.

'What dead man?' she asked.

'The man who was shot dead in Hoddesdon this morning.'

'How do you know his name is King?' She sounded taken aback. 'They haven't released any information yet.'

'Yes, they have,' I said. 'I heard it on the radio at 9.30 this morning.'

Sue was quite nosey and would have been the first person to know. She was adamant. 'Tracy, the next of kin haven't been told yet. No-one knows who the dead man is.'

'Well, I'm telling you it's Dave King,' I said. 'And the bloke with him is Kerry or Kelly.'

Two hours later she phoned me and said they had just released the name of the person who was killed this morning.

'So it wasn't Dave King, then,' I said, expecting to be proved wrong.

'Yes, it was Dave King.' She paused. 'Tracy, how the hell did you know that?'

'Because it was on the radio,' I said.

In the days that followed I spoke to a lot of people, including some who had worked in and around the gym and who had been listening to the radio that morning hoping to hear some news. None of them had heard a name mentioned.

It was while I was spending time studying at the Arthur Findlay College that it happened again. I was driving back one Sunday night, having been at the college for their weekly service, and I was listening to Heart FM on the radio.

I was also on my mobile, hands free with headphones of course. (A friend of mine's brother was killed in an accident involving a mobile phone, so I'm always very careful.) I was chatting away with my friend Laura, who was also listening to the show. We were having a laugh and trying to predict which song would be played next.

We lost our connection, so when I got back home I rang her again.

'That was really sad, wasn't it?' I said.

'What was sad?' she asked.

I explained that after we had been cut off they'd announced that Richard Whiteley had died. I heard the news at 8 p.m.

'What are you talking about?' She sounded confused.

'You know who I mean – everyone loved him. That man from *Countdown*.'

She knew who he was but she didn't know what I was talking about.

However, an hour later there was an announcement to say Richard Whiteley had died just after 8 p.m., the exact time that I'd heard it being talked about on the radio earlier, which was weird.

Laura phoned me and said, 'It's just been announced as breaking news'.

It seemed that the spirit world had given me the news in advance.

The same thing applied to television.

I didn't usually watch soap operas on television. But

I'd begun to see how the spirit world would sometimes use them to give me signs and messages. The first time it happened was when I was doing readings at 'The White Witch' on Saturdays.

That Friday, I got home from my accounting day and flopped on the sofa, exhausted. I sat in front of the television, not really watching it. The Australian soap *Neighbours* was on, and I just let it wash over me. However, I noticed that this episode featured a character who was running a pub and his girlfriend was going to be in a production of *Hello Dolly*. There wasn't much else going on in the episode and after a while it began to get on my nerves, so I switched it off.

The next morning when I greeted the first client of the day something amazing happened. As she sat in front of me, I saw the youngish woman who had come for a reading transfigured into another woman, a much older woman, her grandmother. It was exactly the same thing that had happened to me at that first circle with Barry. The woman's face was completely covered by that of her grandmother, who was wearing a big Russian fur hat.

While this was happening all I could hear was the song *Hello Dolly*. 'Your grandmother is here and she's singing *Hello Dolly*,' I told her.

Sometimes the songs in my head led me towards a name but in this case I didn't feel it was doing that. I could see a stage and I could see this old lady standing on that stage.

I kept getting flashbacks to the episode of *Neighbours* from the night before and the poster that had been on the wall of the pub, advertising the musical version of *Hello Dolly*.

I continued, 'I'm getting the feeling your grandmother used to be on the stage and appeared in *Hello Dolly*.'

The lady looked shocked. 'She was in one of the original productions in the West End,' she said.

I'd barely recovered from that when my next client arrived.

When I began the reading, her mother came through. It was a very strong connection, full of energy. As it grew stronger, I began to hear the *Neighbours*' theme tune.

'What's going on this time?' I asked myself. I sensed a direct Australian connection, and told her so.

'Yes, I do have a connection,' the client confirmed.

'I think your mother must be a *Neighbours*' fan,' I said.

My client looked at me oddly.

Her mother kept showing me a character I'd seen on the programme the night before. His name was Lou Carpenter. 'She's got a thing about this character, Lou Carpenter,' I said. 'She really seems to like him. Does that mean anything?'

This time her face was a picture. She was dumbfounded. 'The actor who plays Lou Carpenter is called Tom Oliver,' she said. 'That's the same name as the father of my daughter, Michelle.'

If she was shocked, I was completely flabbergasted. It made me realise something that I hadn't appreciated fully until now. The spirit world is always looking for quicker, faster ways of getting messages across. It was using the modern media to do that. If I hadn't been watching *Neighbours* the night before I wouldn't have got either of those messages.

After that experience I made sure I watched the soaps all

the time. As I did so I found they helped me with my gift more and more.

Not long after the Richard Whiteley experience, a man came to my centre for a reading. As I began I felt the spirit of another man very close to him. I felt it was his brother. And again I heard a theme tune of a soap opera, only this time it was the other Australian show, *Home and Away*.

It was clear to me there was another Australian connection here. As this connection deepened, the brother began to show me images of beaches and the Australian coastline. 'Yes, he lived there,' the man confirmed when I mentioned this.

'He is also showing me the character Beth from *Home and Away*,' I said. 'What's the significance of Beth?'

'I don't know. I don't know anyone called Beth,' he said.

His brother then started showing me something from an episode of *Home and Away*, involving the character Beth. I remembered it well. It had been broadcast a couple of weeks earlier. I could see Beth in a car on a winding mountain road and the car being hit by a huge articulated lorry. I saw her car going under the truck and her dying.

When I described this to him he looked ashen. He shook his head slowly and whispered, 'That's how my brother was killed out in Australia'.

Today I know how to interpret what I am being shown by the spirit world in cases like this much better than I once used to. Again, this story is an example of the spirit world giving me a vocabulary, a way of interpreting their messages quickly and in a way that everyone can understand.

There was a time, for instance, when if someone showed me the character Harold from *Neighbours*, I knew that it was probably connected to the fact that the character had prostate cancer.

As things like this continued to happen to me, I began to understand something profound. I realised that the spirit world is trying to communicate with us all the time. And the spirits are constantly looking for new and quick ways to get their messages across. As I developed I began to see that, where I was concerned, they would use every available medium, so to speak.

Being a medium in those early days certainly wasn't easy. Despite the success I was getting, there were huge highs and lows. There were still times when I had my doubts. And there were still those who doubted my abilities – and were willing to question them publicly.

Towards the end of 2005, when I felt like everything was falling into place at last, I attended another residential course at the Arthur Findlay College. It proved to be one of the most upsetting experiences of my life.

The course was run by a very prominent medium. He had been trained by Gordon Higginson who, as I'd discovered when I'd worked with Mike Hunter, is regarded as a god by many mediums.

Mike, with whom I'd had such a great experience a few months earlier, had recommended that I did some sessions with this medium. He told me that this man could bring out my mediumship and train me. I had been looking forward to the course for weeks.

It was daunting. Once again I was thrown into a group of people I didn't know. However, I was used to this by now and I understood it was part of the learning process.

On the first morning I was asked to do some stage mediumship. It started well enough, I thought. Normally I can work with energy alone, but in this case while I was standing on stage I could see a father standing next to his daughter. It was so clear; it was unmissable. Inwardly I think I said a little 'thank you' to the spirit world for helping me out.

From the energy he was giving out, I could tell he was a lovely man. The daughter didn't seem so nice, however. At one stage I actually thought in my mind: 'How can you be her father?' Her whole energy seemed so negative.

I pressed on with the reading all the same and began describing the man. It was then that I realised I was going to get a hard time. 'He's American,' I said.

'You know that because you've heard her speak and she has an American accent,' the medium said. As it happened I hadn't spoken to the lady at all. And I didn't really want to.

'OK, you've got a picture of this man in your bag with you,' I continued. 'He is wearing a red T-shirt or polo shirt and a baseball hat. He has beautiful blue eyes. He is leaning on a bar and I can see water.'

'No,' she said.

'It's in your pocket, I can see it,' I protested.

By now the medium was telling me that I had the wrong person, that I was talking to the wrong recipient. This was really infuriating because I could see the father standing next to his daughter as clear as daylight. Again, I would have assumed that he could see this too.

'He's there – can't you see him standing next to her?' I snapped.

The medium looked at me sharply and I thought, 'I've done the wrong thing now.' I had challenged the tutor, which wasn't good news.

I was still standing there on the podium. The tutor sniffed and told me that I had to work mediumistically, not clairvoyantly. 'You don't have the spirit world with you,' he said at one point, which I found really hard to take, especially given there was a spirit standing a few feet from me.

I know now what he was trying to do. He was from an old school of mediumship, one that requires mediums to work in a very disciplined and specific way. But I simply wasn't that kind of medium. I knew that already from my Tarot readings. I did things my way. And it worked. I wasn't a square peg that was going to be rammed into a round hole.

I was really upset by the end of the morning's session, especially when I challenged the American lady later. It turned out that she did indeed have a photograph of her father with her. It showed him in a location overlooking a lake and he was wearing a T-shirt. She claimed that she wouldn't accept my evidence because the T-shirt was, according to her at least, maroon rather than red.

I left the room distraught.

That morning almost undid all the good work I'd done in the previous six years. I'd gone into the classroom feeling really excited. Since being told about this medium, I had been in awe of him every time I'd seen him in the corridors of the Arthur Findlay College. I knew he was very tough but this encounter was all too much for me. He didn't rate me at all.

During the break I went out into the long hall and started crying my eyes out. I think all mediums are – by their very nature – sensitive souls. My emotions were running high. I thought, I'm not meant to be doing this.

I was sitting there feeling sorry for myself when Tony Stockwell came down the main staircase into the long hall. He saw me and asked me what was wrong.

'I'm not going back in there this afternoon,' I said. I then just blurted out all that I was feeling. 'He's trying to get me to work his way, but I can't work like that. I don't know how to do it like that. It doesn't work for me,' I said.

Tony consoled me, letting me get the frustration and hurt out of my system. He knew how hard things were for me. I had taken up more accounts work trying to earn the money we needed to get out of Wormley. It was just too hard. And it was costing me a lot of money just to be there.

'Am I not supposed to be here?' I asked him, calming down. 'Shall I just go home and give up?'

'No, you mustn't give up,' he said firmly. 'Don't be afraid. Get back in there and you show them what you're made of this afternoon.'

I can't say I enjoyed the rest of the day, because I didn't. I don't hold any grudge against the guy. He is a fine medium, someone who has dedicated his life to spiritualism. But in hindsight the episode taught me that there is no benefit in trying to make people work in your way. When I teach other people, I try to be a guide not a dictator, which was what I'd felt this man had been in that classroom.

I passionately believe that the spirit world works with every single person in a different way and you have to bring that out. You can't put people in nice tidy boxes and say to them, 'This is how you must work.'

The impact of that experience might have lasted longer if it hadn't been for the fact that I was booked on another course days later. This one was again at the College but under the tutorship of another well known medium, Leah Bond.

In the days following my disastrous class with the male medium I had seriously thought about giving up. I seemed to be so different from most of the people who were studying there. I really didn't feel I fitted into their idea of what a medium should be.

In the end, I had gone along to the college partly because it was such a lovely, restful place to be and partly because I had paid the money for the course so it would have been a waste not to. The boys were with their dad so it was supposed to be kind of a holiday.

Leah, however, quickly put me back on the right track.

Leah isn't on television or anything like that – but she should be. People should know who she is. It's not just about her mediumship; she is just so warm. You can't meet her and not love her: she is a beautiful soul.

When I told her what had happened the previous week with the well known medium she immediately reassured me. 'You've got wealth all over you,' she said. 'As soon as you stand up you can see the light with you. You're a medium.'

I respected her and I worked really hard for her. By the end of the week I had got my confidence back. I'd also decided it was time for me to make the next big step.

9 | Centre Stage

As I flicked through the pages of that week's *Hertfordshire Mercury*, it didn't take long to find the advert. It was in bold type on one of the inside pages and read:

AN EVENING OF CLAIRVOYANCE
WITH TRACY HIGGS, PSYCHIC MEDIUM

7.30 p.m. The Priory, Ware. Tickets £10

For a moment or two I read and re-read the ad to make sure the details were correct. As I did so, the reality of what I'd done began to sink in. 'What have you let yourself in for this time?' I said quietly, shaking my head.

After the roller-coaster ride I'd had that autumn, I'd decided to take the bull by the horns and stage my first public demonstration. My reputation was building now. I had appeared in *Spirit & Destiny* magazine a couple of times, and I had a steady stream of clients, as well as a regular twenty or so members of my circle.

After my experience with Leah Bond and with the encouragement of Tony Stockwell, I had summoned the courage to take the next step. Even if it was only friends and family, a small public demonstration would be good experience. It would also tell me whether I really was cut out for stage mediumship.

The venue I'd hired, The Priory in Ware in Hertfordshire, was more than 650 years old, dating back to 1338. It had been an army hospital during World War I but was now popular for conferences and wedding parties. I'd been there a few times and loved the energy of the place.

The evening was going to be a big gamble. Hiring the hall had cost £250, while the advert in the *Mercury* had cost another £100. I'd also printed a few flyers, which I'd distributed in local beauty salons. In all I'd spent around £400. I was going to charge £10 a ticket, so I needed to sell around forty just to break even.

To be honest, I'd decided that breaking even would be a success in itself, and anything more than that would be a bonus. If I sold out I'd be absolutely ecstatic!

The *Mercury* came out on a Friday morning. I was still doing readings during the daytime, so I spent the rest of that day with my clients. To my amazement, when I returned home that evening the answer machine was clogged up with requests for tickets. Most had seen the advert, although a few had come across the flyers.

I recognised some of the names from my circle and the teaching classes I was running locally. There were also a few people who had known me when I'd worked at 'Charmed' in Cheshunt and who had since lost touch. But I didn't know many of the names. It wasn't just going to be full of people I knew. I was delighted.

I spent Saturday answering the messages and sending out tickets for the demonstration. By the end of the weekend we'd sold almost all the available hundred seats. I was chuffed.

The euphoria didn't last long. It was soon replaced by a feeling of sheer terror. How was I going to pull off a demonstration in front of one hundred paying customers?

The nervous knot I could feel in my stomach didn't go away during the weeks leading up to the demonstration; if anything, it got worse. By the time the night of the demonstration arrived, I was absolutely petrified.

James had been really helpful in the lead up. He had started studying music at a local college and had helped me put together some music for the evening. He was with me as I drove over to the Priory, although I was pretty sure he'd much rather have been anywhere else. All the same, I was so nervous, I shouted at poor James all the way there.

When I got to the Priory I checked that all the preparations had been made, then sneaked a look at the small crowd of people milling around in the foyer and bar area. A few minutes later, as I stood outside the hall waiting to make my entrance, I was shaking like a leaf. A million thoughts flew around my head: 'What if it doesn't work? What if it all goes wrong? What if I let down these people who have come to see me? Why have they come to see me?'

The state of my nerves wasn't helped by the fact that I hadn't really planned an act as such. I'd seen the professional shows that 'The Three Mediums' put on but, to be honest, I hadn't thought about my stage performance at all. I was more concerned about making sure I was in my zone and that the spirit world would be able to come through.

The only thing I'd really given some thought to was my outfit for the evening. My attitude generally was that no-one would care if I appeared in jeans and a T-shirt. But I realised that people were paying for an evening out to see me. I was a professional now and I had to look like one.

I didn't want to be underdressed but I also didn't want to be overdressed. So I had gone out and bought a black trouser suit and a smart white shirt. I had also had my hair dyed a darker shade, to look more serious. 'But would anyone take me seriously?' I found myself thinking, as the panic deepened.

Fortunately I didn't have any more opportunity to dwell on what might happen. It was soon time for the show to begin.

'Hello, my name is Tracy Higgs, thanks for coming,' I said as I stepped out to the front of the hall, trying not to take in how many people were crammed into the room.

I began by explaining what I wanted the audience to do. I asked people to stand if I was directing a message at them. I also asked them to keep the atmosphere light. 'It's meant to be enjoyable so keep your energy up,' I said. 'If you get bored or lose interest and the energy drops, I'll be rubbish and it won't happen – and it will be your fault!'

There was a ripple of laughter across the audience, which encouraged me. Laughter raises the energy and that means there is more for me to work with. If people get sad their energy drops. It's that simple.

I started with some straightforward card readings because I wanted to get my energy and confidence up. So we handed out a few Native American medicine cards. I then read the cards and read the person psychically in a light-hearted way, which I hoped would get everyone going and bubbling a bit.

It was a mixed audience, about ten per cent of which were men. One of the first people to get a medicine card was a really big bloke. I told him something about his recently starting to do exercise to lose weight. 'But you don't need to be psychic to tell that you need to be doing that,' I joked.

He took it in good spirit, thankfully.

As I went through this part of the show my energy was building so that soon I was ready to burst. I remember feeling that if I didn't start giving this off, I was going to pass out. My energy was so high my head was hurting.

I had all these different spirits saying, *'I'm here, I'm here. I passed with cancer, I was run over in an accident, I passed with a heart attack...'* I was hearing it, feeling it, smelling it – everything.

This was one of the first lessons of the evening. I simply didn't know how to manage things yet. I had to start doing my messages.

When I'd tried stage mediumship at the College I'd made two connections in the space of fifteen minutes. Tonight I was planning on doing two solid hours of mediumship. Talk about being thrown in at the deep end.

Now, because I know what's going on, and I know the spirits can be more patient, I take the messages one at a time. But that night I wasn't doing it and holding back. With so much going on in my head, it was little wonder that the first hour of the show flew. Sixty minutes seemed like six seconds.

Early on I passed on a message for a father and a grandfather. The mother and daughter were in the audience.

'He keeps showing me a Burma star – and it's more than that, because he keeps showing me Burma. I can see a machine and hear noises like an intensive care ward around me and I know he can't breathe before he passes,' I said.

I was being directed to a lady and her daughter in the

audience. The lady's name was Judy. Judy confirmed that her dad had been on a life support machine before he passed so they were the noises I was hearing. She also confirmed that he had won the Burma Star medal during World War II.

'It feels like more than that, though,' I insisted.

'Yes, well, he married someone from Burma,' Judy said. 'My mother was Burmese.'

That brought a round of spontaneous applause from the audience. Back then I was often frightened to mention names. But that gave me confidence. Inside I was feeling rather pleased with myself. Not bad for a first go, I thought. I couldn't rest on my laurels though.

By the time we broke for an interval after an hour I was feeling good. I had done a good job and the audience was buzzing.

I wanted the energy to stay high so I also went into the bar area and queued with everyone for my drink. As I stood there I realised that they were all staring at me. Suddenly it dawned on me. They were probably used to going to spiritualist churches where the mediums were kept at a distance, hidden away in a darkened room. They were getting closer and more personal access here than they were used to.

I wasn't bothered by this at all; in fact I was pleased at their reaction. I wanted to be different. I wanted to be a more modern type of medium. I liked the idea of establishing closeness with the audience.

There were familiar faces in the crowd, including family members I hadn't seen since I was twelve years old. My cousin Rene, a daughter of my dad's brother Norman, had seen the advert and decided she was going to come along. And there were also twenty or so of my students.

Reassuring as it was to see familiar faces, I was relieved that there weren't too many of them. It's harder work when your audience is made up of people you know.

I didn't want to use the energy of tonight to deliver messages to my friends and the people I saw regularly, and had explained this to the audience at the start of the show. I told them that if their relatives came through I would tell them who was there and arrange to talk to them when I next saw them.

As the second half got under way I felt more and more confident. In fact I felt so confident that I decided to let the audience in on my secret.

There was nothing in my advertising that suggested this was my first ever show. I had toyed with the idea of putting something about it being my 'world debut' but thought better of it, in case it put people off.

'That's a relief, you all came back,' I said to warm laughter. 'I'm going to tell you something now, and don't expect your money back, because you've had half a show already.'

I could see they were all curious.

I continued, 'I just thought you'd like to know that this is my first public demonstration.' I was stunned by their reaction. They all stood up and clapped. I nearly cried.

It was amazing. I expected them all to say: 'Oh bloody hell, and we paid a tenner for this.' But they were lovely.

My energy was still really high so the second half also went in a flash. It was over in what seemed like a few minutes, and I absolutely loved every single one of those minutes.

There were some memorable messages again. As the

audience had returned for the second half I'd spotted a woman and her daughter walking in to take their seats. As I watched them it looked to me as if they were walking down the aisle. The daughter was walking behind her, which was weird. She sat in the first or second row to my right. As she did so I realised I was seeing the other figure in that familiar negative.

Sure enough a mother came through at the start of the second half and I felt the energy being directed towards this lady.

'I've got to tell you that I thought you were walking down the aisle. It feels to me like you've recently got married.'

The woman started to cry.

'Your mum's here and your mum's showing me that she was at your wedding.'

This produced fresh floods of tears. It turned out her mother had passed in June and this was only September.

'She is talking about your daughter being a bridesmaid. You've got a lovely man.'

Her mother told her that although she hadn't been at the wedding physically she had been present in spirit. By now, the woman was sobbing. As I told her more, I explained that her mum should have been alive for the wedding. She had bought her outfit and everything, and when she died shortly before the wedding they buried her in her new clothes.

The daughter agreed that this was what had happened.

When I brought the show to a close I got another standing ovation. As I had a stiff drink in the bar afterwards, I had to admit things couldn't really have gone much better.

Talking to members of the audience, it became apparent

that a lot of people had failed to get tickets. We could probably have sold the place out twice over.

The response to the demonstration was so positive I immediately started planning another one at the Priory. Again, we sold out.

Some spirits contact us directly, via messages or even by physically appearing before us. Others communicate with us more subtly – by giving us signs.

I believe we get signs from the spirit world all the time. Often they are from those who are watching over us, our guardian angels. Over the years I've had signs from many people who have passed over, but the one who has showed me the way most often is my grandad Stanley, my father's father.

I hadn't really thought of his presence before I'd become aware of my gift. But he'd been there at the very beginning, when I first went to see Terry Eagletree, who had told me about the incident when I'd cut myself at the time my grandad had his first heart attack when I was fourteen.

Since then, however, he'd become more and more of a presence. And he would show himself in all sorts of ways.

Before I'd moved into the hostel I'd gone round to my nan's house to store some of my stuff. There wasn't going to be enough room for it in the hostel. I'd been very nervous about moving there and I was worried what it would do to the boys.

At my nan's house, I felt my grandad was there again when I went into his old bedroom. In the room, there was an old wardrobe. Drawn towards it, I asked my nan if it would be OK to take a look inside and she said yes. When I looked inside, I saw an old oriental willow-pattern plate. It was the dinner plate that he always used to have his dinner on.

There was also a framed picture of a dragonfly. I believe in the powers associated with different animals and have always been attracted to dragonflies because they represent truth. (It's why the centre I run today is called 'Dragonfly'.) I asked my nan if I could have the picture and she said I could.

I had been really worried about moving into the hostel but this incident somehow made it seem less worrying. I knew for sure then that my grandad was around, watching over me, and that he always would be.

He'd been a reassuring presence again when I was working on the television show in west London. I'd always think of him on the way into the studios each morning. I'd drive down a road called Stanley Road to get there and whenever I did I felt his spirit close. I would then feel he was there with me in the studio, being my guardian angel as I did readings live on camera.

In December 2005, my grandad Stanley came through for me again. This time, he was guiding me away from Wormley and towards a fresh start in my life.

Life on the estate had continued to be a nightmare. I still couldn't park my car without worrying what was going to get smashed next, and James was constantly running the gauntlet of the gang that roamed around.

So when I was told about a cottage for rent on a farm in the small Essex village of Stansted Abbotts I couldn't resist having a look. The night before I was due to visit, a member of my circle said she felt my grandad's presence. 'He is saying that if you see him there, you will know it's the right move,' she said.

'All right,' I said.

When I went to see the cottage I fell for it immediately. It was in a lovely setting, quiet and clean and cosy. But as I looked around the rooms I could see no sign of my grandad.

A lot of women head straight for the kitchen but I'm not that kind of girl. Instead I made for the bedrooms and the bathroom and the living room first. However, there was no sign of my grandad there. But then, as I finally checked the kitchen, there he was.

The kitchen had a lovely Aga-style cooker, and it had the manufacturers' name written on the front – Stanley.

That was it. I knew this was the place for us.

Finding the cottage showed me that my grandad was busy being a guardian angel again. Moving home had a profound effect on both James and me. I was thirty-five years old and it was the first time in my adult life that I felt like I was at home.

Instead of looking out – through drawn blinds – at a faceless housing estate, now we looked out over green fields and what seemed like new horizons. There were deer and pheasants in the garden all the time. It was so peaceful. It was a sanctuary.

After being in that awful flat in Wormley where I would jump up at any noise, no matter how innocent, the only sound I could hear on the farm was silence. It was amazing.

I really did feel as if I was making a fresh start, and I was also able to find a place in the village where I could do readings and run classes. For James too it was a great move.

This was something like the tenth place we'd lived since I'd separated from his father. Given the amount of moving we'd done when we were attached to the Army, it was something like the twenty-first home he'd had since being born. For him too, it was great to find some peace at last.

As we settled into life there I became more grounded myself. I became more sure of what I was doing and the direction I was heading in. I felt like good things were going to happen. And – slowly – they did.

My reputation as a medium had spread quite widely now thanks to my demonstrations, my courses and my regular appearances in magazines such as *Spirit & Destiny*. My diary was always full at my new centre in Stansted Abbotts and I was also being asked to do private readings. Once again, however, I had new lessons to learn.

Around this time I did a reading for some very wealthy people in London. A lady called Olivia, whom I knew through a friend, had invited over a group of her friends for some readings at her home, a huge house not far from Hyde Park in central London. I didn't know who else was going to be there. Olivia didn't tell me anything, which was the way I preferred it.

When I arrived, I was shown into a rather grand drawing room where Olivia told me a series of ladies would come in for sittings. As I made myself comfortable, the first lady came in and sat on a beautiful *chaise-longue*. I couldn't help noticing she was carrying a bag of clothing with a really well known name on it.

Almost immediately when we started the reading I sensed

her mother with me. 'I've got your mum here,' I said. 'She keeps showing me that bag of clothes you have. She's suggesting that's her name as well, although it's not really her name.'

The lady looked at me, giving away nothing.

I went on, 'Her real name begins with E. Something like that.'

Again the lady didn't react.

Despite this I was getting quite a strong flow of information from her mother, who seemed a very forceful character. She continued to give me a lot of information about herself and her daughter.

'Your mum passed of cancer,' I said. 'You've got a daughter here and you've got a daughter in the spirit world. Your father is there as well.'

'Yes,' the lady said, almost questioningly.

At the mention of her father I felt the energy go very low.

'I feel like your father was responsible for his own death,' I said.

She just nodded.

I paused. 'Your dad committed suicide,' I said.

'Yes,' she said quietly.

As her mother continued to communicate through me I also saw a lot about her daughter's personal life but I sensed she didn't want to hear about it that day; it was rather messy. Before I could continue with the reading, she put her hand up abruptly and just said: 'Can you stop now.'

'Sure,' I said. 'What's wrong?'

'Everything you've just told me is correct, but you could have found any of it – well almost any of it – by just Googling me,' she said.

'Sorry?' I said. 'How would I have Googled you? I don't know who you are.'

'Really?' She sounded genuinely surprised.

'Really,' I replied.

She then told me her name. Her surname was the same as the name on the bag of clothing.

'Oh, I see, that's a coincidence.' I smiled. 'That's why your mum is showing me the name on the bag.'

'No, it's not a coincidence. My mother was the lady whose name is on the bag. She was a famous fashion designer.'

'Oh,' I said. I had heard of the designer. She was very well known, although I had to admit I didn't know she had passed over.

We parted on good terms; indeed she contacted me again afterwards for another reading.

As the day wore on I had to tread equally carefully with some of the other ladies, again because of their connections to other famous people.

As I read for one very glamorous blonde woman, for instance, I found myself talking to a man. He had been an actor and was well known for his comedy roles but, as is so often the case with funny people, he had suffered from terrible depression too.

It turned out the man was a very famous British comic and actor and that this woman had played a significant role in his life. Again, she seemed not to believe me when I said I didn't know who she was.

By the time I did the final reading, for another very well

heeled lady in her fifties, I was beginning to wonder what was going on.

She, it turned out, had been married to another great British actor. A Welshman.

Music had been the key to my placing him. He kept singing all these Welsh songs and I was hearing Tom Jones's *Green Green Grass of Home*.

She seemed very agitated and insecure as I passed on what he was telling me. He kept trying to get the message through to her that he really did love her. It was very odd. Again, I think she thought I knew who she was, which I didn't until someone told me afterwards.

The whole experience left me feeling uneasy. Olivia told me afterwards that everyone had been very pleased with their readings, but that wasn't the point. I learned there that I didn't really enjoy reading for celebrities, especially when they were uncomfortable about my knowing who they were. I would tread very carefully in the future.

There were exceptions, of course. As I became better known I read for a well known actor who appeared in a TV soap opera. We met at a masked party, which I'd been invited to by a close friend in Essex.

This guy kept coming over and asking me who I was.

'I'm not telling you who I am until you tell me who you are,' I said.

He was messing around but he was very nice. 'Don't you know who I am?' he said.

'You look a bit like a bloke off the telly,' I teased. In the end I gave in. 'I know what show you were on,' I said.

He was expecting me to say the soap opera but instead I said I knew him from a children's programme I used to watch years earlier. His face lit up at that and after that we clicked. He liked the fact that I wasn't in awe of him.

We started talking about spiritualism and mediums. Within a few minutes I was reading his palm. He wasn't on TV at the time, but was concentrating on running a business instead. He was adamant that he wasn't going back to acting, especially on the soap opera that had made his name.

'You're going to be back on TV,' I said.

'No, I'm not,' he said. 'I've had enough of that.'

'I think you are,' I said. 'You're going to do some weird reality programme and then you're going to go back to doing drama. Not the one you were in, although you will be back in the show that made you well known.'

No matter what I said that night he wouldn't accept it. But it all panned out the way I predicted. At the end of that year he went into one of the big reality shows, which really raised his profile again.

I watched him in it thinking, 'See – I told you so'.

And he eventually ended back on the show that he had started on – just as I had predicted.

The more I developed my gifts, the more I realised I had to have rules that governed how I used them. For instance, I believe in telling the truth. I won't lie.

Everyone laughs at me when I tell them this, but I have this vision of what is going to happen to me when I die.

There is a famous scene in the film *Airplane* where a girl is screaming hysterically and the aircraft crew start slapping her across the face repeatedly. In my mind, if I get to the spirit world, having told lies in this life, then the people waiting for me on the Other Side are going to start slapping me like that woman in *Airplane*. It sounds crazy, I know, but it's what I believe, and it's why I'll always tell the truth.

That said, I have learned, obviously, to be careful about how I put things, but I trust the spirit world will give me things that people can cope with and that are important to them.

That trust was being rewarded on a regular basis now. Late in 2005, as we approached another Christmas, I did a couple of readings for two very different people.

One was the daughter of a woman for whom I'd read almost exactly a year earlier. The mother had been terminally ill and had asked me how long she had left to live. I had told her that she would be here for Christmas Day but not for New Year. So she should make the most of it.

On 28 December, 2004 she passed. I sensed her spirit that night, telling me she had crossed over to the other side. I felt no sadness, only gratitude that I'd been able to help her live her final days to the full.

Her daughter had been so pleased with what I'd done for her mother that she'd become a regular client. On this particular day we were sitting in one of the larger rooms I have for readings. She was talking about going away for Christmas. She had a house in Portugal so I assumed she was going there.

'Going to the house on the Algarve, are you?' I asked.

'No,' she replied, 'we're going to go to Thailand instead.'

I immediately got a strange feeling. 'I don't know why, but all I can see in my mind is water,' I said.

I had a crystal ball that sat on a shelf nearby. When I looked at it, all I could see was an image of a turtle drowning in water. It was really strange. I'd never experienced anything like it before. I thought for a moment. 'I'm sorry but I don't think you should go away there at Christmas,' I said. 'You'll be safer in your house in Portugal.'

Because she trusted me after what had happened with her mother, she cancelled the holiday.

However, her husband wasn't very happy with me at all. He'd been looking forward to the trip with his four sons and his wife. However, on Boxing Day he was very happy to have followed my advice because otherwise they would have been right in the middle of the tsunami.

It was bizarre because I warned someone else off going to Thailand too. It was someone I knew from my days at the psychic television station. She had split up with her fiancé but they were going to get back together again, and were thinking of going to the Far East for Christmas.

Again I got a bad feeling. 'Wherever he is going, it doesn't feel right,' I told her.

She didn't want to listen. 'It will be fine,' she insisted.

I'm not a mad woolly medium, who screams and shouts. But on this occasion I did. 'Please, no – don't go!' I said, raising my voice so loudly it made her jump.

Her fiancé did go out there and he did find himself in the middle of the tsunami. Fortunately he survived.

The other thing I had a strict code about was money. I believe it's important to have rules like this. I wouldn't be able to do what I do without them.

What I do isn't about the money. I have a number of clients for whom I read regularly for nothing. To me, a person who has saved £5 a week for a couple of months to see me will always get the same priority as someone who rings me up, offering me to name my price.

I also don't read for children under eighteen. The only time I'll allow them into a reading room is if they have lost a mum or a dad and they have a relative with them. I certainly wouldn't want to look at their life psychically and tell them where their life is going. And I'm appalled at the number of so-called professionals who believe this is acceptable.

A couple of years ago I organised a charity fair with some friends. A family came up to me and asked me if I would read their daughter's palm. I was reluctant because the girl was quite young, around twelve or so. But then they told me why they wanted a reading. 'This other palmist read for my daughter and told her that she wouldn't live past the age of twenty-five,' the father told me.

A few thoughts flashed through my mind. Firstly, why would you as parents allow someone like that to do a reading for your child? Why have you let that happen? But also what sort of psychic or medium would put things in such a way? The parents couldn't – or wouldn't – name the person who had done the reading, otherwise I would have let them know exactly what I thought of them.

The problem was that I could see the little girl was carrying it. And so I agreed to do the reading only because I needed to repair someone else's damage. I had to help her get rid of this feeling of being cursed.

I said to her, 'No matter how long you live, you – like everyone else – will return to the spirit world at some time.

There's no evidence I can see that you're only going to live to twenty-five.

'But regardless you have to live every day of your life to the full. It doesn't matter whether you live for twenty years, fifty years or eighty years; if you have lived and loved and touched other people's lives then you're all right.'

After we had spoken, I could see the cloud lifting off her.

10 | Bright Lights

In August 2006, Tony Stockwell asked to have a quiet word with me while I was working at his studios in Wickford in Essex. 'Don't know if you'd be interested,' he said, 'but I've got a television company coming in. They're looking for mediums for some new show they are putting together.'

I had never really been that interested in returning to television, especially after the bad experience I'd had at my first television company. 'What's the company?' I asked.

'They produce Colin Fry's television series, *6ixth Sense*,' he said.

I was impressed; *6ixth Sense* was a show in which Colin brought messages through to a studio audience and it was absolutely ground-breaking for mediums. For us to have somebody on television, standing there giving messages from the spirit world to people who would never set foot in a church, was a truly amazing development. Along with shows such as *Psychic School* and Derek Acorah's *Antiques Ghost Show* and *Most Haunted*, *6ixth Sense* was something exciting and new. We had never seen anything on television like that before, portraying what we do in a positive light. I, for one, wasn't surprised when I was told that their television programmes were popular around the world.

I had actually tried to make contact with them before when I'd been with my old agents. I had sent them my details but nothing had come of it. And so I'd thought nothing more of it.

'Well, I see no harm in coming along,' I said. 'To be honest, I'd like to see what they're up to, to if nothing else.'

I didn't really take it seriously. As I settled into life in Stansted Abbotts, I was running classes and doing readings at the new centre I'd established in the village. I was also doing a regular feature called 'Ghost Hunter' for *Spirit & Destiny* in which I went to people's houses to see whether they were haunted. In addition to that, I was writing pieces for *Fate & Fortune* magazine every now and again. It was good for me. I was in the public eye and it was raising not just my profile but the profile of mediums generally. I always tried to do a good job and, I think, succeeded in the main.

Since doing the first two demonstrations at The Priory, I'd continued to do small-scale demonstrations. It wasn't that I didn't want to do more of them, it was simply that I didn't have the time to organise them.

I had done one demonstration at the Corn Exchange in Hertford because I knew the owner, who was keen to have me there. And I'd also been tricked into doing a demonstration at a spiritualist church.

It had been quite funny.

It was in a church near Birmingham and a friend had organised the evening. She told me that it was a demonstration for a group of ordinary, non-church people but the moment I arrived I knew it was a church gathering.

I was standing at the front of the church, when they told me that I should lead them in a prayer. I just thought to myself, 'Oh my God, what am I going to say?' I was miked up and I'm sure they heard me whispering to myself.

So I just said: 'All I want you to do is send up your love, send up happy thoughts and just pray that I do a good job.' The audience was laughing but the church officials sitting in the front row were looking at me as if to say, 'Who are you?'

I'd met one of them when I'd been getting ready in a room at the back of the church. I had taken my shoes off and was jumping around, trying to get my energy up. This man came in and said: 'What are you doing in here?'

'I'm just getting ready, I'm the medium.'

He gave me the dirtiest look. I thought it was quite funny. So I just carried on.

Ironically the first message I got was for him. It was from a father who had had a lot of emotional problems with his son. The son turned out to be him. I learned later that he was the head of the church. He cried during the reading, which was quite intense. At the end he came up to me and simply said, 'Well done.'

The experience only reinforced something that I was becoming more and more convinced about: you had to do your own thing and go your own way.

I kept telling myself that as I headed to Tony's studio that evening.

I knew that I was probably going to be the least experienced medium at this event. So I didn't get my hopes up.

When I arrived there was a lady from the production company who introduced herself as Claire Baylin. She was sitting there with two other lady mediums.

I walked in just wearing jeans and a summer top. The other two mediums looked at me as if to say, 'You aren't going to wear that, are you?' I had a suit in my bag but they weren't to know that.

They were both blonde, good looking young women. I knew who they were. They had both been working for many years on platforms in churches. I also knew that they had probably done ten times as many demonstrations as I had but I wasn't particularly bothered. I was going to be me. And if I wasn't who this production company wanted then I didn't care.

A lot of people are desperate to be on television. But I had turned down television projects because I didn't want to do them. My agents would send me along to things, but – after the experience I'd had in the past – I would always make sure I asked about the concept of the programme before agreeing to an audition.

The success of Colin Fry's show *6ixth Sense* meant that there were a lot of companies out there trying to copy what this production company had done. A lot of them were very amateurish. And a lot of them were doing things that I really didn't like. On more than one occasion I'd said: 'Sorry I'm not interested.' They'd looked at me baffled and said: 'But you're going to be on TV.'

I didn't care. I didn't just want to be on television. It wasn't the be all and end all. I was more interested, as I am now, in trying to help people and in doing a good job. I also wanted every other medium in the world to do a good job. I knew I wasn't the medium for everyone. We need lots of different types of mediums out there. It's the Heinz factor – we need 57 varieties of us in the world.

There were only two or three varieties at the gathering this evening, however.

I got changed and sat in on the other demonstrations. The two girls were the first to take to the small stage that had been set up in the studio. I knew how they worked, which was very different from my approach.

There were three people in the room, sitting there almost like the members of the panel on *The X Factor*. One was Claire Baylin, and I had a good idea who the other two were. The rather elegant dark-haired lady was Hilary Goldman, the head of the production company. The man alongside her was her husband Craig, who ran the company with her.

I knew from my agents that Hilary had a reputation as a really tough businesswoman. She knew what she was doing. But the image of this hard faced dictator wasn't right at all. She was lovely. She was very casual, all dressed in black, with beautiful long hair.

As the evening got under way the two blonde mediums began. They did their stuff in quite a traditional, old school way. They seemed to me to be a bit monotone in their delivery and got through things at rather a slow, sedate pace. But they got results. They both produced some good accurate messages, which they placed in the audience of about forty people.

As I watched them I kept telling myself that I was very different and that this was what I had to accentuate when it came to my turn. I had to be me and I had to do it my way.

When it did come to my turn I wasn't particularly

nervous. As I got going I tried to be light-hearted and funny. It seemed to work. Craig Goldman in particular was laughing a lot, although I was slightly worried it was because he thought I was mucking around, which I wasn't of course.

I brought through a couple of messages. The first was directed at a lady in the audience and was from her mother and grandmother, who had connected with me.

It was the second one that grabbed the panel's attention. By now I had learned that if you ask the spirit world for something they often listen. So I asked for something that only the television people might know. I soon began to get something coming through about a man called Stuart. I kept getting the feeling this Stuart wasn't actually in the room but sitting outside. I then got a strong message about him having been asked to write a book.

Hilary, Craig and Claire were looking at each other as if to say, 'How does she know that?' To me, that was the spirit world's way of telling them: 'She's working for us!'

I soon realised the Stuart I was after was Tony's partner. He was sitting outside the room. I knew him but had never read for him. I certainly didn't know he had been talking to Hilary and Craig about working on a book earlier that day in London.

I received a nice, healthy round of applause at the end of my ten or fifteen minute performance. I was pleased with what I'd done. I'd given it my best shot.

After I'd finished, another medium went on. She was an older, more traditional kind of medium who spoke directly to the spirit, a bit like Doris Stokes used to do. But she was a bit quirky as well.

When the demonstration was over a few of us went next

door for a Chinese meal. We had been told that Craig, Hilary and Claire had gone for an Indian nearby. Throughout the meal we were wondering what they were saying and what they had thought of the demonstration.

Although the other women were more experienced than me and I was the baby medium of the four, I thought I'd done a good job. I hadn't let myself down.

To be honest, I was working hard but I knew I was still developing; I certainly didn't think I was ready to go on a mainstream television show. At that point I also really didn't know what they were looking for, so I put it to the back of my mind.

The following week, I got a phone call from Claire Baylin asking me to come in to see them again. 'We want to film you doing something for us,' she explained. 'Can you come to Hilary and Craig's house in Essex?'

'Sure,' I said.

I had had a good feeling about the demonstration I'd done the previous week, but there was something that I felt I needed to do before I saw them again.

I had kept getting it into my head that I should dye my hair. I'm naturally a dark blonde, but I was very blonde at the time. The other two mediums who had been there were blonde as well. In the days following the audition, I got it into my head that I should get rid of the highlights and go back to being more natural, more brunette than blonde.

It was almost like a message from the spirit world. I kept getting the same phrase in my head: 'You don't want to be like the rest.' Still, I thought I'd better check this was OK, so

I phoned Claire a few days before I was due to go over and film with them.

'I don't want to go ahead and do this without asking you first, but would you mind if I dye my hair dark?' I said.

She laughed.

'What's so funny?' I said.

'Hilary has already said that. She said if you did come on board with us she'd want you to be dark-haired. She doesn't want you to be another blonde medium.'

I booked myself into a hairdresser and dyed my hair. At the Arthur Findlay College, where I was doing another training course that week, a lot of people failed to recognise me.

I should probably have been more nervous about this second interview. If Hilary Goldman was going to the trouble of filming me at her house then the production company must have some interest in using me for a programme.

But I really wasn't nervous. I slept like a log every night that week. Again my attitude was that I wasn't bothered: they either wanted me or they didn't. I would do my best and that would be that. If it doesn't happen it doesn't happen, I told myself.

Looking back I can see that maybe my attitude was down to the fact that I'd already been told by so many mediums by this stage that I was going to be on television and seen by a wide audience, that, in my mind, I knew it was going to happen at some point. If it didn't happen now it would happen later. Equally it wouldn't be the end of the world if it didn't happen for me. That wouldn't stop me teaching and being seen as a good ambassador for mediumship, which was – to me – the most important thing.

When I told people this they often gave me a look as if to say: 'Yeah right'. They just didn't get that about me. I didn't see my profession as a competitive one. I was supposed to be a spiritual person and to help as many people as possible. Being the No 1 medium on television or whatever simply wasn't important to me.

It still isn't.

Having said all this though, I wouldn't have been human if I hadn't experienced a few butterflies as I drove over to Essex for the filming. I'd chosen to wear a black outfit to complement my new dark-haired look.

When I arrived the house was quite busy. As well as Claire and Hilary there was a cameraman there, David, and a guy called Michael Zucker.

It was obvious they wanted to film something to quite a high standard. Cameras were being set up and candles were being lit. Also I was told I didn't have enough make up on, so Hilary sent me to the loo to make myself look a little more telegenic.

While all this was going on, Hilary gave me a bit more background on what was happening. She told me they had got a commission for a new television series called *Psychic Private Eyes* featuring three mediums. They had two lined up, but they needed a third.

'We want to see if you can do one of the processes that will be featured in the show,' she said. There was something very reassuring about her. She was clearly someone who knew what she wanted but there wasn't any aggression or arrogance about her. I felt she was someone who respected the people she worked with – and was respected in return.

As the final preparations were made I was still thinking

they wanted me as a kind of guest star – which I thought might be nice.

Eventually everything was ready and they put me in front of the camera. Michael Zucker was going to be the producer on this show and he gave me a few pointers. He asked me to say a few sentences and then to pause. I laughed.

'What's wrong?' he said, looking baffled.

'I'm a psychic; I can't pause. It just all comes out of me,' I said.

But he was very patient and he explained that they needed pauses for the editing process.

'Oh, I'll try,' I said. I was still thinking, 'You're never going to use this so I don't care really.'

By the time they'd finished setting it up there were two cameras set up and various people watching. They then put two envelopes in front of me. This threw me a bit. When I'm working my eyes go all blurred so I had to explain that I wouldn't be able to read anything.

They said, 'No, we just want you to work on these envelopes, psychically.'

Claire was sitting opposite me at the end of a table nearby so that I had someone to talk to. That's what she thought anyway, because in reality, the spirit world was using her to show me things, which was why she was absolutely exhausted by the end of it all.

Soon after I got under way the spirit of a girl came through and was using her. I could see her face on Claire, although she didn't know it.

I put my hand on the two envelopes. I knew nothing about what was inside. I didn't know if there were photos, documents, money or anything else in there. They asked me to work on them and feel into them and to say if I sensed something.

I put my hand on one and it felt really hot.

Suddenly I could see a blonde girl. I could also see her being attacked. It was really unpleasant, frenzied. I saw her lying on the ground, dead. I didn't recognise her, however, which wasn't surprising as I wasn't very good at watching the news and reading the papers.

I kept looking at Claire for guidance. I was suddenly aware of a song that this blonde girl had sung at her grandmother's funeral.

They let me open the first envelope and there was a letter in there. I couldn't read it because my eyes were still blurry, so I put my hand on it and sensed there were a lot of girls in the family. But I also sensed I didn't want this. I wanted to look at her. I could see her on Claire's face, I could see her long blonde hair. I said that I knew the name Sally was important to her, and that the name Anne was important to her.

At this point the name Sally Anne Bowman still meant nothing to me.

When I opened the envelope I saw a photo and said, 'Yeah, that's her'.

I haven't really got a clue what is going on when I'm in the zone. So when they said cut, I just re-adjusted myself.

'Was that all right?' I asked.

'Yes, well done,' Hilary said, remaining businesslike.

She and Claire told me that the photo was that of a girl called Sally Anne Bowman, who had been murdered in Croydon in 2005. It was a particularly nasty killing. She had been a model and they think she had been stalked by her killer; after killing her he had raped her.

As I left Hilary said, 'I'd like you to come in next week and talk to us.'

'I can't I'm going on holiday,' I apologised.

'OK,' she said. 'I'll call you.'

She was as good as her word. I was sitting on a beach in Spain when my mobile went off. 'I'd like to talk to you about your future with us,' Hilary said. 'You must come to see me as soon as you get home.'

I was pleased. I assumed they were talking about a guest spot on the new show. But when I got back to London and went along to the meeting, I discovered they had slightly bigger plans for me.

I arrived at their offices near Canary Wharf and was greeted at first by Hilary, Craig and Claire, and then by Michael Zucker, who appeared from an upstairs office. 'Well done, TJ – we loved all your stuff,' he said as he came in.

'TJ?' I said.

'Oh yes,' Hilary said. 'We thought TJ was a stronger name than Tracy. That's a bit Essex isn't it? TJ sounds more like a detective.'

I was to discover that this was typical Hilary. The decision had been made and it wasn't really up for negotiation. I quite liked my new name although it was rather spooky. My ex-husband used to call me TJ.

'Right, I need to explain what I want from you in this series,' Michael said.

'OK,' I said, a bit puzzled. I felt like we'd jumped straight into the middle of the meeting.

'The TV show *Psychic Private Eyes* is going to be thirty-three per cent Colin Fry, thirty-three per cent Tony Stockwell and thirty-three per cent you.'

I looked at Hilary.

'Oh, yes. That's why we've called you in. You're the third medium,' she smiled. Again I saw that this wasn't a matter for negotiation. I was being told.

I think I was in a state of mild shock for the rest of the meeting. Michael took me upstairs and introduced me to the new production manager. Hilary said she'd send me the details of my contract within a few days.

I had to sort it out myself. I didn't have an agent any more as my old agency had ceased to be a talent agency as such. They had branched out into internet radio broadcasting and, although I'd done a show for them, we had agreed we were heading in different directions.

I spent a day carefully looking at the contract then signed it and sent it back.

It was a life-changing moment.

Psychic Detective

Psychic Private Eyes began filming just a few weeks later in September 2006. We were recording fifteen episodes for a cable channel to begin with. The show was meant to be a mixture of murder and mystery in which Colin, Tony and I would use our gifts to solve a series of grim crimes.

We would never be given any advance notice of what we were going to be asked to do. Often we would turn up for filming and be given an envelope with some basic information while the cameras rolled to see what we came up with.

They had obviously liked what I did for my audition with the photographs so I was often asked to do photo readings. Sometimes I would be given more than one and be asked to link them together somehow.

Once more I learned new and valuable lessons, about television as well as mediumship. The hardest thing was presenting a pre-written script to camera. Ad-libbing, as I'd done on the cable television channel, was fine. Coming out with a stream of consciousness was natural for me. But having to remember a very specific sequence of lines and names and events was different. I could never get my words right. I found it very frustrating. Thank goodness we had a really professional crew to steer me through.

The other thing I had to learn was to wait for the cameras to roll before interacting with the spirit world. As ever, I had a habit of going in like a bull in a china shop, so I needed to learn to hold back.

One case we were asked to investigate involved a girl who had died in Scotland. Colin and Tony had done their investigations up in Scotland, and I was to go up later, on my own. I had been in Newquay in Cornwall doing a residential weekend teaching course so I flew up to Scotland. I was so tired I slept on the plane.

The producer Tim met me at the airport and took me to the location.

'I had this strange dream on the flight,' I told him.

'Oh really – what was it?'

I explained, 'I dreamt I had very long blonde hair and everyone was pulling my hair out. I felt like I couldn't breathe. It was as if I was being murdered.'

As I was talking he was going white. 'Stop, stop, stop, wait until we've got the cameras on,' he said.

'OK,' I said.

As we drove along I had a sense that I knew where we were going.

'Are you taking me to the flat where she lived,' I said.

Again he looked ashen. 'Stop it,' he said.

It proved one of the most interesting of the cases we did.

When we reached the location and the cameras were running, I told them that this girl had been from Sweden, she was blonde and she'd been drugged and murdered in a green-coloured flat.

The police said that it was a suicide but there was no way it was a suicide. For a start all her hair was missing; it had been cut off. Why was that?

I had also dreamt that I was sliding off a seat because I wasn't tall enough to sit on it. And as I slid off I could smell diesel or vehicle fuel.

When they did their contributions Colin and Tony picked up on this sensation as well. It turned out that the girl had been found near an airport, close to where a truck had stopped.

On the mediumship front, the most pleasing aspect for me was the number of different techniques I was able to use to obtain information. I had been working on using music as a way of interpreting spirit messages, for instance.

The first time I'd really used it had been when I very briefly dated a paranormal investigator. We were driving along one night when I told him how his mum had passed. He said that until I told him her name he wouldn't believe me.

'Her name was Barbara Ann when she lived in England, but it was Maxine when she lived in America,' I said.

He nearly crashed the car. He couldn't believe it. 'How on earth did you know that?' he said, stunned.

'I got it from the radio. I had the song *Barbara-Ann* by the Beach Boys going round my head,' I told him.

I was able to use this method twice in *Psychic Private Eyes*. In the first case, I had to get some information about a boy called Leon simply by looking at a photo of his face. The moment I saw his picture I heard the Bon Jovi song, *Shot*

Through The Heart, And You're To Blame. In an instant I saw that that was how he had been killed: shot through the heart. And he had been.

In another case I kept hearing Michael Hutchence of INXS singing. The music coincided with a message from a guy on the spirit side who was called Michael. It turned out that he had died in very similar circumstances to those in which Hutchence died. He had hung himself with a belt.

I also had to do some weird and upsetting things during the course of the series.

One case that stuck in my mind was that of a schoolgirl called Moira. It was one of the hardest things I had ever had to do.

She was killed by a paedophile.

A lady called Sandra believed that her dad had murdered Moira. She didn't know what he had been doing when the murder happened, or even if he was in the area. Our job was to see whether there was any evidence to support this. Was there anything to link them?

I was again asked to do the photo reading. I was shown a photo of the girl and nothing else. I knew nothing about the man. I was getting nothing at first, which was agitating the producer. I began to feel the pressure.

'I don't know, I'm not getting anything here,' I said.

The minute the cameras stopped I saw the school bus from *The Simpsons* in my head. And I could see this big steering wheel. 'He's a bus driver, a school bus driver,' I said.

Again the producer was so cross.

It turned out that Sandra's dad was a school bus driver and would have picked this girl Moira up on a regular basis.

In an attempt to get more from the reading I was driven

around the town he worked in, Coatbridge, in a mini bus. I did it so that I could have the same experiences. It was horrible, feeling some of the things that had happened to Moira in her final hours.

As if that wasn't bad enough, while we were driving around on the bus I suddenly started getting other images in my mind. They were of the mass murderer, Fred West. I kept seeing his face in my mind.

I later found out that Sandra went to school with a girl that Fred West murdered. What was more, Fred West had lived in the Coatbridge area for a while, which I hadn't known.

It was a tough and emotionally gruelling case. Some of the things I went through were horrible. At the end I felt totally drained. But it had produced a positive outcome, I felt.

Sandra had learned that, as she suspected, her father had murdered this little girl. And that had given her a sense of relief and peace at last, which was what the show was about.

By far the highest profile case we were involved in was the Sally Anne Bowman murder. Our programme on her death drew the biggest audience – and the most publicity to the show. Some of it was good, some of it less so.

Michael, Hilary and Craig were so pleased with the reading I did in Hilary's kitchen for my audition that they actually used some of it in the episode on the murder. But as we looked into the mysterious death I was able to come out with other information as well.

The *Psychic Private Eyes* team took me to the street where

Sally Anne had lived in Croydon. I felt a powerful surge of information the moment I got there. At one point I grabbed my wrist and started saying: 'Marks. I've got marks all over me.' I assumed I was being shown cuts of some kind.

At this point the case remained unsolved.

It turned out the murderer was a man called Mark Dixie.

While I was outside her house I also began to feel details of what had happened to her. I could feel that he had stabbed her and bitten her. I then saw an image of a skip. It emerged that they had found her body next to a skip.

I came up with evidence that hadn't emerged in the course of the investigation. Some of the things I said couldn't be corroborated by Hilary or anyone else, as the case hadn't been to court at that time.

At one point I sensed that one of her sisters, Michelle, looked very much like Sally Anne and she was thinking of having her hair cut off.

I felt Sally Anne's sprit telling me she shouldn't. 'Tell Michelle not to do it,' I said.

I also heard Sally Anne singing a song at her grandmother's funeral.

They sent the DVD off to the family and the sister had an appointment to have her hair cut off the next day, so she cancelled it. Sally Ann's mother Linda apparently demanded to know how I'd known what Sally Anne had sung at her grandmother Mary's funeral. It had been the exact same song.

There was some negative reporting in the press when the programme first came out. Some said we were recreating people's grief for the purpose of entertainment. But that wasn't what the show was about as far as I was concerned. To me it was about helping families in pain. And with Sally Anne's family I think we achieved that in a small way.

I formed a good relationship with the family and Sally Anne's mother Linda in particular.

When Mark Dixie was tried and convicted, I did a reading for her.

I felt Sally Anne's presence very strongly and was shown some photos of her that were stuck to a wall. I could see they were the walls of Mark Dixie's cell in prison. 'He's telling everyone that they are pictures of his girlfriend,' I told her.

She went straight to the prison authorities, who immediately tore them down.

The police weren't always sympathetic to what we were doing on the show. We were looking at cases that were old or left in limbo. They didn't always welcome the scrutiny.

In the Sally Anne Bowman case an officer did watch the episode of *Psychic Private Eyes*. But in one or two of the other cases we looked at they weren't so welcoming.

In my work before *Psychic Private Eyes* I'd come to understand that, quite rightly, the police couldn't have people like me ringing them every five minutes. At the time of the Soham murders, for instance, I had sent thoughts out. I still wasn't a developed medium at that point. All I got was the word 'school' and the word 'caretaker'. I was, however, working with another medium called Sheila and she could also see children in a local school.

So we called the local police where we were. But we were ignored.

The experience put me off ever doing it again. So I don't

do it now unless I'm invited. When high profile cases crop up I keep my head down. I wouldn't get involved unless I was personally asked by the parents.

To be honest, that's where my priority lies in these cases. It's not my job to apprehend the criminals. That is for the police. My job is to help those who have been affected by these crimes to find some kind of peace. Whether it's knowing for sure that a missing loved one has passed over or finding out more about the crime that ended their lives, grieving relatives want closure. And I can help give them that.

This was the reason why I was happy to take on another case during *Psychic Private Eyes*.

Tony and I went to Ireland to investigate the disappearance of a girl. The case had been a controversial one. The mother of the girl who had gone missing, Anne Bourne, had claimed that her daughter had been killed by the son of a prominent public figure in Ireland.

The problem was that there was no body. She had simply disappeared and never been seen again. The police knew about the mother's allegations but it seemed as if they had walked away from the case. They'd said they couldn't help her with it because of where it was going. And so, as far as Mrs Bourne was concerned, they had let this young man get away with murder.

She suspected that her daughter had died while visiting her boyfriend's family farm in the Irish countryside. The *Psychic Private Eyes* team took Tony and me to the area near the farm. We were driving along a road that ran adjacent to the land when we both turned almost simultaneously and looked in the same direction.

'She's over there,' we both said.

We were both convinced this girl's body was buried on that land. We had to tread really carefully, however. This was a very powerful family, and it was a very serious allegation we were making.

We felt even more uneasy when we were told that there was no prospect of the police searching the land. The family involved were simply too influential and the evidence for searching the land – as far as they were concerned – too vague.

Tony and I had to return to Ireland at one point, and we felt very uncomfortable throughout the trip. It was almost as if we were being watched or followed sometimes. It was the first time that I felt like I'd put myself – and my family – in danger through my mediumship.

As 2006 got under way, my career seemed to be on the up and up. I had completed my first major television series and my reputation was growing not just around the UK, but around the world.

The show *Psychic Private Eyes* had already been sold to other countries and I was told that if I went to certain parts of Eastern Europe I might get mobbed in the street. Apparently it was the number one show in Romania – but only when there wasn't any football on television!

Hilary and Craig were already talking about a second series. Bookings at my centre were flooding in, and my classes were packed with a group of really lovely people. I was fulfilling my dream of being a teacher.

I should have been feeling on top of the world. And yet I wasn't – far from it. I wanted to give it all up.

A number of things had cast a cloud over the successes I'd enjoyed.

Firstly I'd become ill towards the end of filming *Psychic Private Eyes*. I'd been experiencing a lot of pain in my stomach area again. It had reminded me of the troubles I'd had with the polycystic ovaries when I'd been younger, but it turned out to be something different. It was my gall bladder.

The doctors ran some tests and told me I'd have to go into hospital for an operation to have it removed. It had knocked me for six. It took me ages to recover my energy levels.

I had also faced a bit of negativity. One or two snide articles had been written in the Press and on the internet when *Psychic Private Eyes* had been broadcast. I should have expected it. By sticking my head above the parapet I should have known I would get shot at by people who questioned the world of mediumship. It was something I know Colin Fry, Derek Acorah and Tony Stockwell had faced too. But it didn't make it any easier to bear. It was a price of fame thing. I'm very sensitive and when people start to attack me I can sometimes go into a downward spiral.

I was also being recognised a lot more. This might sound silly. It wasn't stopping me getting out of the front door. I wasn't being mobbed in the street like David Beckham or anything like that. It was subtler than that. But I just got a sense that people were more aware of me now that I was 'that psychic off the television'. For a while, I'll admit, it made me a little paranoid. I was seeing negativity where there wasn't any.

During a weekend course at the Arthur Findlay College, run by Eileen Davies, the medium who had been so supportive of me in the past, I started getting a particularly negative feeling from one of the other students.

I hadn't really picked up on it until we did an exercise, involving us all being blindfolded and sitting in rows facing each other.

Every time this one particular person sat in front of me I would feel really negative. It was a vaguely familiar feeling, one I'd had before in the past, but I couldn't quite place it.

It didn't make sense. She was a very friendly, rather smiley person. She was Welsh, like Eileen. But I couldn't shake off this negativity that I experienced whenever I was near her.

We were there for the weekend and as the Saturday wore on I became really paranoid that she didn't like me for some reason. It became so bad I asked the other mediums. 'I don't know what I've done to her but the energy I'm getting is really negative,' I worried. 'I don't like it and it's affecting me. Is it because I'm on television and she doesn't approve of that or something?'

One of the more experienced mediums suggested that I simply try to send the negativity back to her. But that didn't work.

I didn't sleep particularly well on the Saturday night. When I went down to breakfast on the Sunday morning I still felt odd. When I turned up in class, there was no sign of her. Someone said she'd been taken ill during the night and wasn't going to join in.

I was so paranoid I convinced myself it was because of me. She disliked me so much she wasn't coming to the class. But why didn't she like me, what had I done? Was it really because I'd been in the media?

I found out that it was nothing to do with me at all.

I heard during the week that the lady passed away on the Tuesday. Suddenly I understood what had happened. I was also reminded of where I'd felt that same feeling before.

When I'd lived up in Yorkshire, before having James, one of the nicest members of my ex-husband's family had been a gorgeous man called Malcolm.

I remembered that the last time I had been around him I had that same feeling I'd had here. I had never worked out why I'd felt that negativity because he was a lovely man and he had always been good to me. The feeling I was getting was that it was as if he didn't like me any more.

I'd never connected that feeling with what happened to him not long after I got married and moved to Germany with Tony. Malcolm had been very proud of his car, a Volvo, and kept talking about how safe it was. 'The safest car you can drive,' he would say.

Soon after I'd left Pontefract he died in a car crash in his Volvo.

That was the feeling I had been getting here. This lady – like Malcolm – had been getting ready to go to the spirit world. They were coming to get them. I had been picking up on it. If I'd been feeling better about myself I'd have understood what it was more quickly. As it was I'd got the wrong end of the stick.

My disillusionment also had a lot to do with the fact I was going through a hard time in my personal life. Again.

It was a while now since I'd had a relationship. I was beginning to wonder whether my career was compatible with having a 'normal' relationship. Trying to be a normal person, doing things like dating, is difficult when you're a medium.

The first thing that men suspect is that you can read their minds. But, after all, you don't really need to be a genius to work out some of the things men think. We are women, we know.

Because of what I do people assume that I can read all their thoughts, that I know all about them, and that I know all their insecurities and all the things that make them feel vulnerable.

I have to deal with all that.

Around this time, for instance, I went on a date with a guy I'd met socially before. We had some things in common; we both loved *Star Trek* and *Star Wars*, for instance.

We had planned to go to a pub, but on the night of our date it was snowing so he asked me if I wanted to have a coffee at his place. He was really into technology, something that can leave me cold. He had a fancy new microwave, which you could scan information into so that the microwave knew how to cook it. It was so boring. He was telling me about this.

I jokingly mentioned that I tended to avoid electrical things, because they went a bit mad around me when I'm working.

I had told him what I did when we'd first met. There was no point in hiding it. I was fairly well known in the area and we had a few mutual friends. He was vaguely interested in it, I could tell. 'If there's someone from the sprit world with me could you see them?' he asked me while we were in the kitchen.

'Yes,' I said. 'But I'm not working at the moment.'

That wasn't entirely true. As I was talking to him I could see his nan behind him. I was trying not to.

He wasn't giving up though and he asked me what kind of things spirits could tell me.

I just did my usual thing and came out with what was in my head. 'Well if, for instance, your nan was standing next to you she might tell me things like your nickname at school, or the fact that you got picked on by other boys for being fat or the fact that you used to wet your bed,' I said. 'That sort of thing.' I was joking, but of course I'd obviously got something right. His face went white. I had a fair idea why.

In his hallway I felt a lot of energy. I was trying not to work. I didn't want to freak him out. But sometimes I just can't avoid it. So after a while I decided I was going to leave. By now I had already come to the conclusion that I didn't want to see him again anyway. I get bored really easily and he was boring me.

The snow was falling quite heavily by now. He did clear the windscreen of my car before I left, which I thought was quite gentlemanly.

When my phone went in the car, I thought it was him again. I was trying to get back onto the A1 and we'd talked about how to get there beforehand. 'That's nice he's ringing to find out if I've found my way,' I thought to myself. 'Maybe I misjudged him.'

How wrong could I be?

'What have you done?' he said, when I put the call to speakerphone.

'What do you mean?'

'I switched on the lights when I got back into the house and the whole electrical system has blown. You're a freak! Why have you done this to me?' he said, verging on the hysterical. 'I'm frightened to go downstairs in case you've left anything else down there.'

I just hung up. He sent me a few apologetic emails afterwards, but I ignored them.

It was funny in a way but in another way it hurt. It made me wonder whether that was what people really thought of me. Did they think I was a freak?

I'd had to put up with this before, of course, in particular with Adam, who didn't like my work progressing. Was a normal relationship beyond me? From talking to other mediums, I knew that a lot of them had gone through this thing where they felt their gift was some kind of punishment.

I was now in my mid-thirties. I looked around me and many of my friends were in happy, stable marriages with children. I had been through a lot of relationships that didn't work.

I began to think that if I was to be a medium then I would have to accept that I was destined to be on my own, that I couldn't be this person professionally and have a personal life too. It almost began to feel like a priest who has to follow his calling. I didn't like the idea.

On top of all this, I had started to feel overwhelmed by the burden of expectation on me.

When you're a medium, so many people need you. At times it's as if your life is for other people not for yourself. People expect you to be superwoman but you're not. If you're ill, you're ill. If your kids need you then your kids need you. But that didn't seem to bother some people.

It was yet another reason for me to wonder whether it was a curse and not a gift.

So as I began the New Year in January 2006 I came to a decision. I was going to close down the centre I now had in Waltham Abbey. I would fulfil the bookings that I had for the next few weeks, and then I was going to stop.

I thought, 'What is the point?' I would do a second series of *Psychic Private Eyes* and then go back to being a boring accountant. At least that way I might get a normal life.

I knew the spirit world wouldn't be very happy about this. They had put a lot into me. They might put some barriers up to stop me walking. But I was sure I knew what I wanted to do. I wasn't going to be dissuaded by anyone – living or dead.

After recuperating from the operation over Christmas I went back into work at the centre in Waltham Abbey on 6 January. I looked in my diary for that day and saw that I had a woman booked in who had been cancelled twice because of my illness.

It was clear from the moment she arrived that she hadn't been happy about it.

'This is my third time of trying to see you, you've cancelled me twice,' she told me as she walked into the centre.

'Please don't have a go at me,' I said to myself. I was feeling really disillusioned. Before I did the reading I said to her: 'If it doesn't work today you will get your money back.'

But even before we had crossed the corridor into my reading room I could see there was a man with her.

No sooner were we in the reading room than I knew who it was. 'Your father is standing beside you,' I told her.

There are times when the spirit world comes through so strongly I barely have to do anything to interpret it. This was one such occasion. This man was so clear I was just listening to his words in my head then repeating them virtually verbatim.

'He keeps telling me the number three,' I said. 'He was in a hospital and in an ambulance. Was that three weeks ago or three months ago.'

'No, three days ago,' she said.

He came in with so much evidence that he even blew me away. And I'm a medium.

He was talking to me as clear as a bell. There was none of the bouncing energy I get sometimes when it's someone who has recently passed. This man was unbelievable.

As he continued to connect with me I began to get the feeling he was telling me off. It was as if he was saying to me, 'My daughter is here for me, so you just bloody well get on with your job.'

But it wasn't negative. I felt as though he was telling me to 'get those doubts out of your mind girl, this is what you're here for'.

I had known the spirit world would have something to say about me quitting but I didn't expect it to come through so soon.

The girl cried almost every minute of the reading. She

clearly had been heartbroken by her father's passing. The emotion of getting a message from him was clearly overwhelming for her.

For some reason the man wouldn't tell me his name. But he did tell me Barbara was his wife. 'Bring your mother next time,' I told her. 'He's saying you must bring Barbara next time.'

I wasn't touting for business, quite the opposite. I was trying to slow the business down. When I looked in the diary I saw that a lady with the same name and address as this girl was already booked in. Her name was Barbara.

Her daughter thanked me profusely as she left.

'That was brilliant,' she said. 'They said you were the person to come to.'

I don't know how she knew but she'd somehow got wind of my plans to leave. As she headed for the door she just said to me: 'If you give this up, my dad is going to haunt you'.

When Barbara came to see me a few days later it was a similar story. This man came through again, as clearly as anything. This time he spoke to his wife about what she'd been up to in the house. The accuracy of his evidence was again mind-blowing.

I kept seeing Roy of the Rovers. He kept showing me the turnstiles at Tottenham Hotspur. It turned out that he worked at the turnstiles at Spurs' ground at White Hart Lane and his name was Roy.

Roy told me that she had put some little red roses by the memorial she has in the garden for him.

As a reading, again, it was one of the very best I'd done. And as she left Barbara was again adamant that Roy wasn't going to leave me be, even if I wanted him to. 'Don't you dare give this up!' she said. 'The only way Roy can talk to me is through you. He won't talk to any of those others,' she added. 'Roy won't forgive you if you stop.'

Both readings left me feeling elated. They completely changed my mood. They had reminded me of what I was capable of doing. And they had also reminded me of the good I could bring into people's lives.

It wasn't long before my spirits were lifting again.

The next time I saw Barbara, she asked me whether I was still thinking of giving up. I just smiled at her. 'No,' I said. 'I'm waving the white flag. Roy and the rest of the spirit world have won. I'm staying put.'

12 | Towards the Future

One night towards the end of 2006 I was sitting in a hotel bar in Cardiff with Colin Fry and Claire Baylin. Colin was in Cardiff to perform in the *Best of British Mediums* show with Tony Stockwell. I'd joined him there to film some promotion material for *Psychic Private Eyes*.

Colin was unwinding over a glass of red wine when the conversation turned to his plans for the rest of the year. As ever, he had a long list of dates already confirmed for his latest tour of the UK and New Zealand.

'I want you on stage with me next year,' he said suddenly looking at me.

I looked at Claire who was sitting there and I just laughed. 'I don't do the stage thing,' I said. 'Especially not in front of thousands of people.'

Colin was insistent, however. 'I want you on stage with me,' he said again.

Before I really knew what was happening, I had agreed to appear as a guest in dozens of Colin's shows up and down the country.

I began by appearing in the *Best of British Mediums* shows in 2007; then in 2008 I appeared as a guest star on Colin's own hugely successful tour of the UK and Ireland.

Working with Colin was great. Not many people get to know him well but I felt I got to see the real man beneath the public persona. For a start he had a wicked sense of humour, which endeared him to me straight away.

One of our first gigs together was at a big theatre in Liverpool. As we did the sound check on the stage I looked out into the auditorium and nearly died. It was absolutely vast.

Colin caught me staring and obviously worked out what was going through my mind. 'No need to be nervous, darling – there will only be two and half thousand people there tonight,' he teased.

It became something of a running joke between us. When we played the Edinburgh Playhouse he caught me looking stagestruck again. 'I hear they've only sold 3,660 tickets tonight, darling,' he said.

On that particular occasion, I cried with nerves. Throughout the early part of the tour I was convinced that I wasn't good enough to be sharing the stage with such a revered and experienced medium as Colin.

During the first few shows I know I rushed my act. I was so desperate to get off stage again. I just went out and pointed at the people who I had messages for. There was no building up the evidence and feeling my way into the audience. I just looked for the lights that I often saw above people who were getting messages and dived in. Sometimes I spoke so fast it was as if I was commentating on a horse race. The audience must have thought, 'What on earth is going on?'

Yet slowly but surely, I began to gain confidence. Again

the key was to be myself and to draw on my own experiences of life.

In December 2007 I got a phone call from Claire asking whether I would like to go to New Zealand on tour with Colin.

I was enjoying the experience by now, so I said yes.

It proved to be a big turning point for me. I did the same thing there as I did in England. But it was a real learning ground for me as a medium. I relaxed more, probably because I thought, 'If these people don't like me then that's fine, because I live at the other side of the world.'

We were about halfway through the tour, however, when we got some devastating news. Hilary Goldman had been hospitalised with pancreatic cancer. She had been first diagnosed the previous January. She had dealt with it admirably and had lost none of her qualities either as a businesswoman or as a woman.

Hilary had become a great friend to me. She really was one of the rocks on which I built my life. She always used to thank me for things I did, whether it was a stage show or a television appearance. She used to ring me and thank me almost every day sometimes.

By the time Colin and I returned to England she was very ill indeed. We were almost immediately back on the road, touring the UK and Ireland again in the spring. It was while we were performing in Skegness – on Friday 24 April 2008 – that she passed over.

We were in the signing queue at the end of the show when

we got the message. We carried on signing; we knew we had to. Otherwise she would have kicked our arses.

We'd assumed because it was Saturday – the Jewish Sabbath – that the funeral would be postponed for a day or two rather than be held the next day, as is the custom.

But we were mistaken. It was only at 9 a.m. the following morning that we heard it was happening that day – in just two hours time, at 11 a.m. We didn't have a hope of getting there.

Colin and I were back on stage that night. It was a strange day for the whole team. We were all quite raw. Before the show began all of us were backstage together. We had chivvied each other along with the old 'the show must go on' stuff, which was true it had to go on, and Hilary of all people would have insisted that it did.

But it was clear we were all thinking about her.

About five minutes before the show began, as Colin was getting ready to step out in front of the packed audience, we were all standing at the side of the stage. We decided to give each other a group hug. All we wanted to do was go home and cry, but as we hugged we told each other that we had to go on. As we did so I said to them all, 'Can you smell that?'

From the ground upwards there was this really strong smell of perfume. I didn't know it at the time but it was Coco Chanel.

Everybody smelled it, even our cameraman Tony and he wasn't a medium. It was clearly her perfume. It was obvious to me that she was there with us.

Colin went on first and then I went on for the last 15

minutes of the show. I was still shaky. I wanted to grieve for this wonderful woman, but at the same time I knew she would have been saying, 'Get on with it'.

As I got ready to go on I also thought if I cry on stage I'm going to let the crew down. Colin, in his usual very thoughtful way, said he would stand in the wings watching over me.

My head was spinning. No sooner had I stepped out on stage than I had a mother with me. The initial connection, once more, was being made via music. The song I had in my head was *Tell Laura I Love Her*. But as more evidence started coming through I turned cold.

'Oh no, please don't do this to me,' I thought.

It was a woman who had passed in her late forties from cancer. All I could think of for a moment was the fact that Hilary was 46 and had died of pancreatic cancer.

'I don't know if I can do this,' I said to myself.

A lady in the audience put up her hand. When she had the microphone she said her name was Laura and her mother had passed of pancreatic cancer in her forties. It was clearly the right person.

As I'd done so often now I started talking about my own experience sensing that it would also relate to this lady. It did. 'She left behind two children, two girls,' I said. 'She said goodbye to them before she passed.'

As the reading progressed, she was answering yes to everything I was saying.

The more I related it to Hilary the more it seemed to fit this lady's life too. After a couple of minutes of this I couldn't hold it in any more. I was crying my eyes out at this point.

The audience was probably wondering what the hell was going on. As the reading went on I began to lose control of my emotions and was crying quite loudly as I spoke, gulping for air at times.

By now I was looking across to the side of the stage to the cameraman who was filming the shows. 'What do I do?' I mouthed.

Thank God Colin had offered to stand on the sidelines. He rushed on stage and held my hand as I carried on. After a while, he took the microphone and started to speak.

'Ladies and gentleman, there is something you should know,' he said, close to tears himself. 'Our producer and dear friend Hilary Goldman died of pancreatic cancer last night and was buried this morning. She was only forty-six and left behind two lovely children. This is why TJ is having a hard time bringing this message through.'

Well, that started the audience off. I don't think I've ever seen so many people crying at the same time.

I was so grateful to Colin for doing that.

I don't know why I felt embarrassed that night. Part of me didn't want them all thinking I was an attention seeker. But afterwards it started me pondering again about this curious job that I now did for a living.

When grief strikes a medium everyone thinks, 'Oh you're a medium, you're all right.' But we are still human beings. We still grieve for people. We still miss people. Especially when you lose a forty-six-year-old woman who has changed your world and the world of many others.

In the following days, I couldn't stop thinking about Hilary. It was, I realised, the most significant death I'd had to experience since I was a little girl.

When death happens to other people it's my job to bring them through so that their loved ones know that they are all right. People have so many questions. 'Why did I lose my mum?' 'Why was my son murdered?' I'm sure Hilary's children had those questions too. It was my job to answer them.

In this case, though, I had those questions as well. Why did we lose Hilary? Why didn't she survive the cancer? I was very angry about it. She had done so much good in her life – why did this happen to her? It did make me question everything for a while again. It took me some time to separate myself from the emotion and remember that, as a medium, I knew that she was still alive in the spirit world.

I believe that we come here to fulfil our souls. Wherever she is, Hilary can rest in the knowledge that she did a good job. She can put her feet up....

There is, I think, a lot of rubbish talked about spirituality and what makes a person spiritual.

I don't think lighting a candle and putting on a bit of tinkly music makes you a spiritual person. A spiritual person is someone who embraces what they have gone through and tries to do good. I believe that if you do one good thing for another person then your soul will go to the spirit world lighter.

It's going to sound mad, but I believe when I die I'll sit down and I'll watch a film of my life. It will feature everything I've been through, good, bad and indifferent. When it comes to my turn to sit there and watch that film of my life I hope I'll see that I have done some good; being a medium certainly gives me a great opportunity to do so.

It's not always about bringing messages through to loved ones. There is a bigger picture. These people are coming back and telling us that yes, they have had a physical death, but they have not gone. I think this is the biggest message of all.

I remember being young and being frightened when I was first confronted by death. Because of my mediumship I have been able to teach both my children not to be afraid of death or dying. They know that if I go I'll still be there. Every time I help someone in the world realise that, then I feel like my work is worthwhile.

As my life settled down after *Psychic Private Eyes* and touring with Colin Fry, I felt like I was in a position to help people more and more. By now I had opened a teaching centre in Waltham Abbey. After years of basing myself in various places – from 'Charmed' to 'The White Witch' to Stansted Abbotts – it was good to get what seemed like a permanent home.

Nothing gives me greater pleasure than working and teaching. The centre isn't a business; I don't see it like that. It's simply a place where people can come and counter all the negativity about psychics, mediums and spirituality generally. They can find themselves there and they can be themselves there.

I have faced so much negativity myself, often because I've never done things the old school, traditional way.

I never dreamed I'd get it, but I always wanted a place

where people could come in and – no matter what they believed in – they could be part of a spiritual experience.

A lot of other good things came out of the newfound profile I'd been given by television and a national tour.

For one thing I'd been reunited with my father – again. We hadn't fallen out or anything like that. But since I'd been in the hostel and suffering from depression, there had been a distance between us once more. It's just the sort of thing that happens in families.

To be honest, it was largely of my making to begin with. I had deliberately stayed away from him when I'd been really low. Like all families I suppose, they had a unique gift for saying the wrong things, so I'd thought it best for both sides if we didn't see each other.

Then, as I'd got more and more into my work as a psychic, I'd avoided them for other reasons. Back in the early days, when I was at 'Charmed', my dad had made it pretty clear that he didn't really agree with what I was doing for a living. But as far as I was concerned nothing was going to get in the way of my using my gift and doing what I was meant to do. I suppose I was being the stubborn teenager again, looking back. Deep down, I'd known that I couldn't meet up with my dad again until I'd proved that I was right and he was wrong. And that time had arrived.

The great thing about me and my dad was that we always let bygones be bygones. I knew we'd be able to pick up where we'd left off if I made contact. So when I woke up one morning over Christmas 2006 and decided I was going to go and see him, I knew he'd be pleased to see me.

Getting in touch with him wasn't quite as straightforward as I thought it would be, however. I drove over to the house in Enfield and discovered they'd moved. They hadn't left a forwarding address either. Typical, I thought.

I don't know whether it was a guardian angel, perhaps my Pops, watching over me, but within days the spirit world was giving me a helping hand.

One morning I was looking out of the window of my centre in Waltham Abbey when I saw a guy walk past. I knew him from years ago; his name was Carl. I knew his dad was friendly with mine. Perhaps he might know where my dad was living. I ran out and shouted: 'Carly, is that you?'

'Yes, hi Tracy, how're you doing?' he said.

We had a quick catch up chat and my dad soon came up in the conversation. 'Your dad's doing well with his pub up in Cambridge, isn't he?' Carly said.

'What?' I said. 'He's taken over a pub in Cambridgeshire?'

'Yes, I went up there with my dad. It's "The Plough and Harrow" near Ely,' he said.

'You haven't got a number for him, have you,' I said. 'I've lost it.'

'Sure,' he said. 'I'll bring it round in a minute.'

To his credit, he did.

I was so excited. I had so much news to share with my dad. I was much stronger and more confident about things now. There was so much going on in my life, with the television series in particular. I also wanted to give them some warning that I was going to be in the public eye, which might have some impact on them.

Silly as it seemed, somewhere deep down inside me I also

didn't want one day to write a book like this one and end it with the phrase 'I don't see my dad any more'.

When I rang my dad his first words were, 'Oh, you got my message then?'

'What do you mean?'

'I came into your shop last Thursday, but you weren't there. The girl in the shop said you were out filming,' he said.

'What, you left a message with the girl in the shop that you'd called?' I said, ready to fire the girl immediately.

'Well, no, I didn't exactly. I just thought she'd mention that some bloke had been in looking for you. I thought she'd work out it was me.'

My dad does bear some physical resemblance to me, obviously, but I wasn't paying my staff to be psychic about every dodgy looking bloke that walked into the shop.

'So it wasn't a message at all then,' I laughed.

'No I suppose not,' he said. I could feel the ice melting immediately. The next day I was sitting in his pub having lunch. That's the way it always was with me and my dad. Unlike my mother, with whom I'd barely had contact again since finding her, we would see each other, give each other a hug and put our past differences behind us in a moment. And that's the way it will always be, I know.

It turned out that he and Heather, my mum, had been following my career all along. They knew all about me appearing on *Richard & Judy* and *The Xtra Factor*. They even knew that I was going to be filming *Psychic Private Eyes*, from a small piece in a local paper.

It was wonderful to see them again. It's funny sometimes how it takes a long break away from someone to open your eyes to some things. There was a moment over lunch when I saw dad look at Heather and Heather look back at dad, and I thought, 'I would like to be loved like that one day'.

In a way, even though I was now nearer forty than fourteen, it was the first time I'd looked at them with adult eyes. Their attitude towards my career had completely changed. After I'd had something to eat my dad jumped up and said: 'Right, go behind that bar and tell me what you feel'.

Heather shot me a look. 'He's been having experiences,' she said, rolling her eyes.

As I walked along the corridor that led to the front bar I tripped and almost fell over. I could see the spirit of a Jack Russell terrier.

In the bar I sat on a stool. 'There's a man who sits here, he's called Graham,' I said. As I sat there a little longer I felt really cold. 'You must nearly freeze sitting here,' I said to my dad.

His face was an absolute picture.

I then looked around the bar and saw a little lady. 'There's a little lady here who knocks over the menus on the bar. Her name is Mary,' I said.

There was a family having lunch in the restaurant that had lived in the village for many years. My dad went over to them laughing his head off. 'You won't believe what my daughter's just said,' he said. He thought it was hilarious.

But the smile soon faded. As he told this family about what I'd sensed they began nodding. 'Yes, that's right, Graham was landlord here many years ago. He always used to sit on that stool,' the mother said, before adding, 'His wife was Mary.'

My mum also told me that the menus were often falling off the bar for no apparent reason and that people frequently tripped in the corridor.

'Someone reckoned it was like tripping over a dog,' my dad said. He spent the rest of the day shaking his head in disbelief.

Soon afterwards we had a Ghost Hunting Night at the pub. My dad sold tickets and he packed the place out.

There was a room upstairs in which he reckoned he'd heard noises. There was also a man he kept seeing in the restaurant area. He was bald and wearing a suit, according to my father. I sensed his presence too. I told my father he might be psychic himself, which made him laugh.

Epilogue

A lot of people tell me they would like to do what I do for a living. I always encourage them. Everyone is psychic, I think. We are all intuitive, we all know things. It's just how far you go with it. How far you trust it. Some of us are Monets, painting lovely, colourful landscapes and some of us are Lowrys, drawing simple matchstick men. That's the way I look at it. We've all got a different way of working.

Having said that, however, I really do believe that you need to have lived a life before you can be a truly successful medium.

I believe you need to have a bulk of life experience to be able to go out there. You need to have felt those universal emotions that people feel every day – grief, pain, pride, regret, guilt, happiness, love and all the rest. You need to have them stored up in your mind, almost.

I count myself as incredibly lucky to be able to do the job I do. But I also know that, without the experiences I've had in my life, I wouldn't be able to do that job as well as I do.

The more I work and travel, the more convinced I am that there was a purpose to those experiences. They happened for a reason. It's not just the range of emotions I've experienced that has helped me. All the different people I've met and places I've lived in have played their part too.

Years ago, for instance, I read for a young guy in his early twenties. He was a tough-looking lad with short hair.

It was all still quite new to me so I was mainly concentrating on Tarot and psychic readings. If I got a mediumistic presence as well it was a bonus.

Pretty quickly I was aware of the presence of an elderly lady. It felt like it was his grandmother. It turned out she had passed quite recently. This was why he had come to see me. Her presence wasn't very strong and she began to fade. As she did so another set of images began forming in my head. They were very familiar to me.

'I can see you standing in the streets of Belfast, in a full military uniform, with a gun,' I said. 'You've served in Northern Ireland.'

He snapped forward, looking shaken. 'How do you know that?'

'I just do,' I said.

He really didn't look pleased. 'You're looking at my soul,' he said. 'I didn't give you permission to do that.'

I told him that he had – actually – given me permission. 'By sitting here in front of me you're giving me permission,' I said. 'But if you want me to stop I will.'

'No, sorry,' he said. 'It's OK. Carry on.'

As I focused on the energy that I was picking up on I began to experience a lot of the emotions I'd been through while living in Londonderry. I felt fear and mistrust. I felt terrible pain and guilt as well. Soon I began to sense another person's presence.

'There's someone else here, a man,' I said. 'He died a violent death but he is at peace now.'

I could see the guy's body language tightening. I was soon getting a really strong feeling that he was somehow connected to the man.

It was clear to me that the person on the other side wasn't a soldier. I was a bit apprehensive about saying what I was beginning to feel. 'You were there for his passing,' I said.

'Yes,' he said quietly.

'He died from gunshots. You fired the gun.'

'Yes.' He nodded just the once.

From there on it became a very emotional reading. I passed on the message that the man was at peace and that he understood what the ex-soldier had done. It had been an act of self-defence. If he hadn't killed the gunman, the gunman would have killed him.

It was an exhausting reading. I felt drained by the end. The guy shed tears, as I did.

We chatted for a bit afterwards and I told him about my experiences living in Londonderry. He told me that it was the first time he'd talked about it with anyone since leaving the Forces. He said he felt as if a huge weight had been lifted off his shoulders.

'I did what I had been trained to do, not what I wanted to do,' he said. I told him that if Tony, my ex-husband had been in that situation, I was sure that's what he would have said.

Since then I've often found myself connected with the spirits of those who have served in conflicts like Iraq, Bosnia, Northern Ireland and Afghanistan. Talking to other mediums, it seems to happen to me a lot more often than it does to them.

One night, performing on stage in Kent, I was doing a 'double link' with Colin when a career soldier came through. He was trying to get through to his wife, who was in the audience.

I began picking up on some images that were very familiar from my past, from the time I lived in Germany with Tony.

'I'm seeing NAAFI stores,' I said. 'I'm feeling like I'm in Germany. In the town of Hohne near Hanover.'

'Yes, yes, that's right,' the woman said excitedly. 'We were stationed at Celle and used to go there shopping together.'

Her husband had been killed in Afghanistan and wanted to get through to her that he was at peace. Colin and I were able to give her that assurance. Colin was able to give her some other information, but because of my particular experience with the Army I was able to give her something more concrete.

If I had not lived the life I had, I would not have been able to do that, I would not have been in a position to give that lady the true feeling that her husband was there.

At some point or another, almost every experience I've had – sometimes good, more often bad – has proven useful in my work. I'm sure the few that haven't will do so too before my days as a medium are over.

A couple of years ago, for instance, I did a reading for a lady privately. Her nan had passed over and she wanted to see whether I could bring her through, which I did. As the reading went on, however, I was beginning to wonder whether there were any real problems in this lady's life. The picture I was getting was so rosy.

I sensed that she had a wonderful husband, a strong marriage and a lot of nice people around her. When someone like that comes to see you, you inevitably think, 'What's the problem? Why has she come to see me?'

I was soon to discover the answer. I began experiencing sharp pains in my stomach. One of the stabs was so sudden it made me wince.

'Are you OK,' she asked, concerned.

'Yes, fine,' I gasped. I had recognised the pains immediately. They weren't the type of thing you forgot. I just looked at the woman and said: 'You have polycystic ovaries.'

She looked absolutely stunned. She then burst into tears.

Now I knew why she had come to me. She had exactly the same condition that I'd had after having James. I immediately felt sympathy for her. I was reliving the pain all over again and it was excruciating.

As things began to fall into place, I also knew why her nan had come through so strongly. The lady was terrified she wasn't going to be able to have a child. Again, my own experience meant that I could imagine what she was enduring.

It was her grandmother who helped put her mind at rest. 'She's showing me a baby. She's saying you're going to have a child,' I said.

Again the tears flowed. But I could tell she wasn't happy at this.

'No,' she said, shaking her head. 'The doctors have told me I can't. We've been trying for three years.'

If I'd felt that she wasn't going to be successful in having a baby I would obviously have told her. It was my duty to be honest, in as compassionate a way as possible.

I had in the past done readings for women who were desperate to have children and been absolutely honest with them. I remember one lady was going through her third or fourth round of IVF and was absolutely obsessed with getting pregnant. But, hard as I tried to get the spirit world to help me, I couldn't see it happening. And, sad to say, it didn't.

I was having no such difficulty here, however. There was no doubt in my mind she was going to conceive. I couldn't get away from the fact that her nan was showing me a baby.

'I can see you holding this little boy,' I said. 'It's going to happen.'

As a woman and a mother I could see the situation was killing her and probably harming her marriage. When I suggested this she told me that she couldn't talk to her husband about it. Again, I understood. Tony hadn't been the most emotionally communicative man either. There had been times when I'd been pregnant with Ryan when I'd felt desperately lonely.

'I'm afraid my marriage is going to break down,' she cried.

I really didn't sense this happening, though. And the more I connected with her grandmother the more convinced I was that she was going to have a baby. 'I'm being shown the date 20 January. You will have a baby around that date. Your baby will come early but it will be OK.'

It was eighteen months later when I next saw the lady. In the days beforehand I'd had a dream about her holding a baby. I was walking across the car park in Stansted Abbotts when I saw her pulling up in her car. I waited for her to park, then approached her.

'I was dreaming about you last night,' I said. I looked

inside her car and there was her baby boy. He had the most amazing beautiful blue eyes.

'It was all just as you said,' she laughed. 'He had been due on the twenty-first of January, but he was born a month premature.'

In those early days I used to record my readings. Legally I'm no longer allowed to do so. I had given her a tape of one of her readings. She told me that she and her husband had listened to it repeatedly during her pregnancy. 'It helped us a lot,' she said. 'It gave us faith that it would all work out in the end. And it did.'

Again, it was an example of me using the experience I'd had myself with Ryan to help others. If I hadn't gone through the pain of my own operation and the uncertainty that followed it, I wouldn't have been able to understand and reassure her. It just underlined my belief that everything in my life had a purpose.

I believe the spirit world operates on a very personal level. It conveys messages through mediums by using and interpreting the unique emotional vocabulary each of us has in our minds. When you think about it, it makes perfect sense. Why make us speak in a second language when we can get the message across better in our first language? Why make us use references that mean little or nothing to us when we can get the message across much better by talking in terms of things that refer to our own lives and experiences?

Of course, this means that the richer the emotional vocabulary a medium has the richer and more powerful that medium's messages are going to be. The more you store in your mind in terms of experience, the more you're giving the spirit world to work with.

I've had such a varied life. Sometimes I think I've led the life of three or four people. I've had so many rich, emotional relationships, with family, friends, a husband and two sons. I've been through so many experiences as a child, a mother, a wife and a human being. Often I go back to where I grew up and I see people who have been doing the same jobs, living in the same houses with the same partners for twenty years, since they left school. There is nothing wrong with that, of course. But I'm glad that I've lived so much of a life.

I'm glad because everything that I've done since I arrived in this world – good and bad, and there's been a lot of both – is now being used to help people. As a medium I can now, in a sense, recycle the huge range of feelings I've experienced to benefit others who are going through similar emotions.

So I now know that my life has had a purpose. The things that have happened to me have happened for a reason. As a result I now feel complete; I believe I have filled that hole that I once had inside me.

There were a lot of times when I felt very differently. For a long time I thought my life was cursed. But I don't think that any more. Now I know it's blessed.

It's a gift.